DREAMS TO REALITY

A PIVOTAL YEAR IN THE HISTORY
OF WIDNES VIKINGS

Mike Healing

Trafford
PUBLISHING

To my wife Lynn
&
Tony, Sue, Anton, John and Christine for introducing me to the game, and their company in the North Stand.

In memory of Pauline

Acknowledgements

The idea of writing this book came from my role as statistician for the Vikings' Matchday Programme. The compilation of those statistics, which are reproduced in Appendix IV, was only made possible through the generous assistance of club statisticians across this country, Australia and France. I thank them all.

For their encouragement and support throughout this project I am indebted to my wife Lynn, my friend Bob Greaves, and Paul Cook, author of The Cook Report in the Matchday Programme.

In addition the contribution of Paul's interviews with Steve McCormack has provided a wider perspective on life at the Halton Stadium.

I must also thank long-standing Vikings supporter Dave Anslow for his perceptive artwork, along with KT8 Photography and the Widnes Weekly News for the inclusion of their images, and October Communications for their promotional support.

Valuable assistance was also received from Steve McCormack, Pat Cluskey, Peter Knowles, the Runcorn & Widnes World, Kay Johnson Gee (Administrators), the Rugby Football League (Operations, Media and Officials Departments) and Paul Smith Associates.

The finishing touches were kindly provided by valuable contributions from players past and present, fans, Derek Twigg MP, and members of the media.

Thank you all.

PICTURE / ARTWORK ACKNOWLEDGEMENTS

Contents

Foreword   ix

Abbreviations   xi

Introduction   xiii

Chapter 1   **Replay**   17

Chapter 2   **Warm Up**   25

Chapter 3   **Kick-Off**   39

Chapter 4   **Half Time**   85

Chapter 5   **Second Half**   101

Chapter 6   **Extra Time**   167

Chapter 7   **Final Whistle**   183

Chapter 8   **Press Conference**   201

Chapter 9   **Administration**   221

Chapter 10   **A New Beginning**   245
             Profile of Steve O'Connor   262

Chapter 11   **Factfile**   265

FOREWORD

I think it's fair to say that the 2007 season was one we will all never forget.

We will look back with fondness on some tremendous victories – none more so than the Northern Rail Cup final at Blackpool against Whitehaven where we were roared home by thousands of ecstatic fans.

But we will be less inclined to remember with any affection the Grand Final where Castleford ended our hopes of promotion to Super League.

Then there was the trauma of administration, followed by the re-birth of the club and the promise of better days ahead.

Personally, I am delighted to be back with the Vikings after it looked as if my association with the club had ended and I know the players are also looking forward to whatever challenges the 2008 season might hold.

I hope this book serves as an interesting reminder of the ups and downs we encountered in 2007, and I'd like to thank all the fans for the support they showed us during the season.

Steve McCormack
January 2008

Abbreviations

CCC	Carnegie Challenge Cup
NL1	LHF National League One (2006)
	Co-operative National League One (2007)
NRC	Northern Rail Cup
NRC-KO1	Northern Rail Cup – 1st knockout round
NRC-Q/F	Northern Rail Cup – Quarter Final
NRC-S/F	Northern Rail Cup – Semi-Final
NRC-Final	Northern Rail Cup – Final
RFL	Rugby Football League
App	Starting appearances
Sub	Substitute appearances
M	Total Match appearances inc. substitutes
T	Tries scored
G	Goals scored (Drop Goals in brackets)
Pts	Total points
P	Played
W	Won
D	Drawn
L	Lost
B	Bonus points
F	Points For
A	Points Against
Diff	Points difference
N1	Neutral Ground - Blackpool
N2	Neutral Ground - Headingley
Att	Attendance
HMRC	Her Majesty's Revenue & Customs

Introduction

Attending a family party would not normally be described as a life-changing experience, but for this author that's the way things turned out. The 'day after the night before' became a landmark in my sporting life when it was suggested that we spend the afternoon at the Halton Stadium, watching the Vikings take on arch rivals Warrington. From a position of never having seen a Rugby League match I found myself hooked, moving on with indecent haste to become a season ticket holder, sponsor and (minor) shareholder!

In the intervening five and a half years I have soaked up a rare mixture of facts, rumours, anecdotes and the obligatory conspiracy theories to add to my limited knowledge of the bygone 'glory days'.

As the 2007 season dawned I, like many others, bought into the anticipation and excitement that surrounded the club, and first had the idea of writing this book. From its inception the book was intended to record, from a fan's perspective, a dream journey back from the relative obscurity of National League One to Super League rugby. As we all now know this dream was transformed into a nightmare of epic proportions, particularly for those more closely involved than us 'mere fans'. Whilst the pain was real enough for us who support the club it was all the more acute for those whose careers and livelihoods were affected, by events outside their control, whether they were office staff, players or coaching staff.

Whilst the outcome of the season was demonstrably not that which was expected or hoped for, this book is intended to serve not only as a record of the 2007 season, but will hopefully act as a prompt for each and every one of us who took part in the journey, to recall our own personal memories and anecdotes of a season that will, I believe, be seen as a watershed in the history of this world-famous club.

That journey unwittingly began in Warrington as the Vikings' faithful trudged, heads bowed, away from the stadium on that miserable, wet October evening in 2006. On their way back to Widnes the fans experienced emotions ranging from disappointment to abject despair as their team fell at the final hurdle. Unhappily Head Coach Steve McCormack was experiencing this feeling for the third season in a row, and those of us on the outside could only guess at the disappointment felt by the players and staff, but it's a fair bet that at the very least it matched that of the fans. It is also safe to assume that the determination to achieve success in 2007 went up several notches overnight, for those who remained - in both the boardroom and dressing room - as the planning began to return the club to its rightful place amongst the elite of Rugby League.

As Steve McCormack finalised his recruitment for the new season the portents were promising as a squad with more strength in depth, and balance came together, and the season began in a positive vein. When the Chairman resigned in a blaze of publicity on the day that the League campaign began it could so easily have undermined all that had gone before. If anything the opposite was true as the club and fans seemed to become a more close-knit unit, and under the stewardship of new Chairman Peter Knowles and Chief Executive Pete Barrow it stabilised off the field and made significant progress on it.

The tangible reward for progress on the playing front came when the Vikings returned from Blackpool with the Northern Rail Cup, their first senior trophy since winning the Northern Ford Premiership Grand Final in 2001. Ominously the

Sky Sports commentators drew attention to the fact that no team winning the Northern Rail Cup since the Final moved to Blackpool had gone on to secure promotion to Super League. Based on performances thus far, including two momentous wins against Castleford, the Widnes faithful were convinced that their heroes would 'buck the trend'.

Performances did in fact dip after the Cup Final even though the results continued to come -Halifax apart - until a significant defeat in the final home game of the regular season against Castleford. Although this was shrugged off by the die-hards, myself included, it eventually led to the Vikings conceding home advantage in the opening play-off tie, and seemed to hand the initiative to our likely Grand Final opponents.

And so we eventually moved on to Headingley hoping to put to rest the disappointment of 2006, only to witness a performance widely described as the worst of the season. The failure to secure a place in Super League for 2008 was enough to reduce some on the terraces to tears, but there was an even bigger shock awaiting Widnes fans, players and staff alike when the club announced its dramatic decision to enter Administration just two days after the Final.

The next three weeks - a period which seemed more like three months due to the necessary 'news blackout' - was filled with rumour, counter-rumour and a frenzy of activity by the various supporters' organisations who simultaneously felt the need to be doing something positive to help the club in its hour of need. A range of fund-raising initiatives were launched aimed at raising funds that could be passed on to the club when the ownership issue was resolved, while countless ideas were put forward by equally concerned individuals for the effective re-structuring and re-organisation of the club.

Finally on 1st November the waiting was over as the outcome of the ownership issue was announced, and the appointment of a 'new' Head Coach was made. Even then there was another twist as the RFL kept us all on tenterhooks until 19th November when our membership of the governing body was finally confirmed, albeit subject to a 9 point penalty to be imposed for the 2008 season.

The new era of Widnes Vikings was under way. New owner Steve O'Connor had made a welcome declaration of intent when within 24 hours of assuming control he had regained the services of Steve McCormack, and also reversed the decision of the previous administration and given his Head Coach the green light to recruit a full-time playing staff.

From the depths of despair on 9th October, Widnes supporters could now look forward, only six weeks later, to 2008 with a measure of confidence for the future of their team and club.

The following pages chart the events at the Halton Stadium as I saw them unfold during the course of the season, and beyond, written contemporaneously, and not altered through hindsight or subsequent events.

CHAPTER ONE

Replay

National League 1 Grand Final 2006

8th October 2006
Halliwell Jones Stadium, Warrington

Hull KR   29
Widnes Vikings   16

This, hopefully, red-letter day began with the familiar drive from Sale to Widnes, with my Widnes-born wife, where we mingled with the growing number of black-and-white be-decked fans gathering on the platform at Widnes Station. We all harboured desires to return later in the day exhausted and 'high' on success as the Vikings would surely be *'homeward bound'* to the top flight of English Rugby League. We are now only too well aware that the dream was lost on a tidal wave that swept in from Humberside. However, as kick-off time approached I began searching for confirmation that this was indeed to be 'our day'. Thoughts came and went but as the afternoon wore on I was left with nothing more tangible than these, hopefully good, omens:

The Station ticket office was closed, meaning a free ride for all to Warrington;

Hull KR fans were many in number, but seemed so over-confident;

Hemel Stags were in the NL3 Final - I went to school in Hemel Hempstead;

In the NL2 Final Swinton included several ex-Widnes players in their line-up;

'Yorkshire' couldn't possibly win all three finals; and Surely the Gods would allow Terry and Barrie to sign off on a high.

Such is the logic of any sports fan on 'big match day', but slowly one by one these omens vanished into the ether around Warrington, of all places, leaving us with the stark reality that come February we would be kicking off another season in the Northern Rail Cup and National League One.

Like so many Finals in any sport the prize outshone the performance, certainly as far as those of us from Widnes were concerned. Although Hull KR had the edge for most of the game it seemed as though some of the Widnes team 'froze' on the big occasion, and the Yorkshire outfit claimed the prize of a place in Super League for 2007. Their ultimate success was based on a barnstorming start to the match with the Widnes defence struggling to maintain its shape as Hull crossed the line for the first time in the 6th minute, and then cruised to a 16 – 0 lead before Gavin Dodd reduced the arrears for the Vikings. Unfortunately the Robins went up another gear to increase their lead again just before half-time.

Widnes had to score first in the second half to have any chance of getting back into the game, but an uncharacteris-tic handling error by Barrie McDermott early in the second period led to the Robins again crossing the line. Bob Beswick eventually created the space for Ryan Tandy to score, before Damien Blanch added a late consolation effort for the Vikings.

As the rain continued to fall at the final whistle, virtually to a man the Widnes players sank to their knees exhausted and despondent – for some it was to be their last appearance in a Widnes shirt.

The most poignant sight was that of Terry O'Connor, in his last match as a professional Rugby League player, disappointment etched on his face, having failed in his attempt to take his home-town team back into Super League. The 34-year-old front rower had never stopped trying to drive his team forward but his 415th and last game did not have the happy ending that he, and the fans, craved.

Another hurting and reduced to tears was Steve McCormack for whom this was the third consecutive losing Final, having been defeated as coach of Whitehaven in each of the previous two seasons. A proud man who had suffered torrents of irrational abuse from so-called 'fans' throughout the season, Steve was nonetheless prepared to put his head above the parapet only a few days later at the Player of the Year Awards. He was rightly given a very warm reception by those in attendance, as he spoke of the collective determination to go one step further in 2007.

Hull KR:	Cockayne, Rivett, Morton, Goddard, Ford, Murrell, Webster, Aizue, Fisher, Tangata-Toa, Morrison, Smith, Gallagher. Subs: Weisner, Barker, Netherton, Wilson
Tries:	Ford, Goddard(2), Murrell, Weisner
Goals:	Morton (4), Murrell 1 dg

Vikings: Dodd, Blanch, Gleeson, Cardiss, Kirkpat-
              rick, Moran, Watson, O'Connor, Smith,
              McDermott, Cassidy, Allen, Beswick. Subs:
              Summers, Wilkes, James, Tandy,

Tries: Dodd, Tandy, Blanch
Goals: Dodd (2)

Referee: Phil Bentham   Att: 13,024

RETIREMENTS

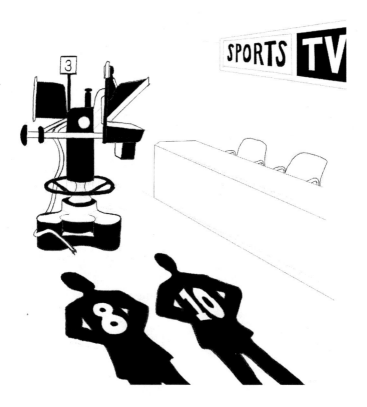

Amongst the departures were two players who had brief but popular stints at the Halton Stadium who had decided that this was the time to bring down the curtain on their illustrious playing careers. Sadly they were joined by an equally popular, but much younger player who had been forced to retire through injury.

Terry O'Connor moved from Wigan Warriors in 2005 to realise an ambition to represent his home-town club before his playing days were over. A veteran of over 400 games, including representative honours for Ireland and Great Britain he was team captain as the Vikings fell from Super League at the end of that season. Being a local lad Terry felt this more than most, and decided to postpone his retirement plans for a further twelve months in an attempt to return his beloved Widnes to the game's top flight.

Coincidentally, at the same time, Terry's great friend Barrie McDermott had opted to end his playing career and moved over to the coaching staff with Leeds Rhinos. As Barrie tells it, "O'Connor mithered me so much" that he finally relented and in turn extended his playing career into 2006 to join the Widnes cause, finishing his career with 367 domestic appearances to add to his representative appearances for Ireland and Great Britain. Together they formed a formidable front row pairing as the Vikings sought to reclaim their place at rugby leagues 'top table', ultimately falling at the final hurdle, but they had become big favourites with the fans through their wholehearted endeavour.

Although they were lost to the game as players, they were to immediately re-invent themselves as an unlikely, but highly successful and amusing double-act as they were 'transferred' to the Sky Sports team as presenters and pundits. Their down-to-earth punditry and 'investigative' pieces on a variety of rugby league issues have been a joy to behold!

Sadly a much younger member of the squad had also been forced to announce his retirement from the game, through injury.

Tim Holmes had made a total of twenty five senior appearances for the club during the Super League era, scoring two tries, before he broke a bone in his neck, ironically in the Testimonial Game held in January 2006 for the former Wigan coach, and Warrington legend, Mike Gregory. After six months of intensive treatment the 24 year-old former Great Britain Students International was able to resume playing. However a recurrence of the injury in a Senior Academy fixture ultimately forced the decision to quit after further specialist treatment. Taking up a position on the coaching staff with the Vikings Tim stated that he was "devastated to finish playing the game I love, especially at my age - I had so much more I wanted to achieve. I feel like I've been robbed", and added "I would like to thank the medical, coaching and office staff and all the boys at Widnes for their support and advice throughout this year, they've been brilliant. I feel privileged and grateful to have been a member of the squad and have made some true friends for life."

At a Sportsmans Dinner held in Holmes' honour in December 2006 'Tez' and 'Baz' gave those fans present an insight into their future career prospects as they hosted the evening with a superb blend of sensitivity and humour. Thinking he was going out for a meal with team-mates the affable fullback was somewhat surprised to walk into a packed Bridge Suite at the Halton Stadium, to find that he was in fact the Guest of Honour at the function also attended by such luminaries of the game as Paul Sculthorpe, Kris Radlinski and Gary Connolly.

CHAPTER TWO

Warm Up

Planning and Re-building

The squad for 2007 started coming together long before the dust had settled on what was ultimately a disappointing 2006 for the coach, players and supporters of Widnes Vikings.

The first 'signing' for 2007 was one that really gave a boost to everyone connected with the Club – Mark Smith. Since signing from Wigan Warriors in 2005 'Smithy' had become a firm favourite of the Vikings faithful with his 'never-say-die' attitude and commanding performances, both in attack and defence. The retention of Smith for 2007, before the final outcome of 2006 was known, was the declaration of intent that the fans were looking for from the management of the Club, and set the standard for Steve McCormack's continued recruitment programme.

Soon 'Smithy' was to be joined on similar 'dual contracts' by other stalwarts from the 2006 squad: Dennis Moran, Jordan James, Damien Blanch and Aaron Summers. On completing his permanent transfer from Castleford Tigers Blanch indicated the growing spirit within the camp when he said: "I've really enjoyed my last few months at Widnes and it wasn't a hard decision for me to make when the offer came. The Club, from players to fans, have been fantastic and I look forward to moving to the area and the 2007 season."

Others to remain with the club for 2007 included the Club's 'all-time record points in a season' man Mick Nanyn - who amassed 388 points in all competitions in 2006 - Bob Beswick, Gavin Dodd, Mick Cassidy and Oliver (Ollie) Wilkes. "Bitterly disappointed to miss out on the final part of 2006" through injury, Nanyn had turned down "more lucrative offers" to pin his colours to the Widnes mast in the drive towards attaining Super League status. Meanwhile his teammate Dodd was moving to full-time status for the first time in his career. Described by his coach as being "one of our most potent attacking forces", Irish International Dodd said after signing his contract: "I can't wait to get back into training and look forward to the new challenges that being a full-time professional will bring."

While Mick Cassidy admitted to having ambitions to move into coaching, he remained at the Halton Stadium on a part-time contract, adding that "I feel I have another season in me and hope to help the Club go one step further than in 2006." McCormack said of his most experienced forward: "Cass rolled back the years in the final months of the season and although he will only be with us on a part-time basis I'm sure his professionalism and will-to-win will rub off on the rest of the team."

While the rumours abounded in Local, National, and Rugby League Press about potential signings, October 13th 2006 saw the Vikings announce the signing of six new players for the coming season. The most well known addition to the squad was Centre Toa Kohe-Love. One of Super League's most prolific try-scorers, the 29 year-old Kiwi from Wellington made the short journey from Warrington, having also played for Hull FC and Bradford Bulls.

Another Centre to join the squad for 2007 was Andy Kirk, who having begun his career at Leeds Rhinos also represented Salford City Reds and Wakefield Trinity Wildcats at Super League level before moving on to Halifax. Following a successful 2006 at The Shay Andy brought his pace to Widnes on a two-year deal.

A large turn-over of the playing staff at arch-rivals Leigh enabled Widnes to capture the signatures of two former Centurions in Dean Gaskell and Scott Grix. Irish International Winger Gaskell, who had been a target for Widnes 12 months previously, finally signed for the Vikings having started his career at Warrington, where he had made 59 Super League appearances prior to his move to Leigh. The versatile Grix joined home-town club Halifax as a 17 year-old, had a spell on loan at Doncaster, and then linked up with brother Simon at Warrington, before establishing his reputation at Leigh. Scott's CV also includes a year playing in France for Limoux.

The No. 7 shirt at Widnes had become something of a poisoned chalice in recent years with fans bemoaning the lack of creativity from this position. There were high hopes that in Scrum half Andy Kain it would be a case of 'problem solved'. Kain was a player who first caught the eye of McCormack whilst he was in charge at Whitehaven. His performances for Castleford Tigers in 2005 led to him being voted the LHF Young Player of the Year and caused McCormack's Whitehaven team no end of problems that season, before the coach finally got his man for 2007.

Finally, on a busy day the formalities of Lee Doran's move from Rochdale Hornets were completed. Second rower Doran, Player of the Year at Spotland in 2005, came to the attention of McCormack with fine performances for the Hornets against the Vikings in 2006 and became a key target for the coach as he sought to re-build his pack following the retirement of Terry O'Connor and Barrie McDermott. Also bolstering the pack for 2007 was Welsh Prop forward Gareth Price. Former 'Union' player Gareth became a professional Rugby League player at 17 but returned to the 15 man code in 2001 when he signed on loan for Neath. The journeyman forward had since worn the colours of London Broncos, Leigh Centurions, Rochdale Hornets, Hull KR and Celtic Crusaders and was "looking forward to joining a big club like Widnes and chose the Vikings in front of stiff competition from a host of National League 1 Clubs".

Home-town boy Paul Noone was also added to an increasingly impressive looking squad. The former GB Academy captain last pulled on the black and white jersey as a schoolboy when he captained the Widnes side before beginning his professional career at Warrington. Having spent the latter part of the previous season on loan at Harlequins (formerly London Broncos) Noone realised his boyhood dream and signed for the Vikings. "I had several offers from Super League Clubs for 2007 and gave them serious consideration but as soon as I knew there was an opportunity to join the Vikings there was no other team for me"

The pre-season rebuilding was completed with the signings of Ian Webster, Andy Bracek and Ben Harrison. McCormack said of the capture of Webster from St. Helens: "Ian comes highly recommended from Saints and I know he is looking forward to pushing a claim for a place in the starting 13 week in, week out." Webster, who can play at halfback, hooker or loose-forward made his Super League debut at Catalans in August 2006, and has signed a 12 month deal with an option of a Super League contract should the Vikings gain promotion at the end of the 2007 campaign.

The twin loan signings of Bracek and Harrison - initially discussed by Paul Cullen and Pat Cluskey when they were away with the England squad - will allow two exciting young forwards to spend the season with the Vikings. These signings were, in no small way, made possible by the contribution from fans' organisation 'Vikings Quids In (VIQI). 19 year-old Bracek had already represented Saints and the Wolves at Super League level, while 18 year-old Harrison had represented both Cumbria and Lancashire, as well as captaining the English Schools team.

In acknowledging the fans support McCormack said: "I would like to personally thank the members of VIQI whose weekly contributions have allowed us to be in a position where we can finance this deal as VIQI will be contributing to the monthly payments". He also went on to praise the officials of both clubs who brought the deal to fruition.

The senior squad looked like this as the first match of the season approached:

Fullback	Gavin Dodd, Scott Grix, Scott Yates
Wing	Damien Blanch, Dean Gaskell
Centre	Adam Bowman, Andy Kirk, Toa Kohe-Love, Mick Nanyn, Matthew Strong
Half Back/Hooker	Andy Kain, Martin Keavney, Dennis Moran, Mark Smith, Ian Webster
Prop / Second Row	Andy Bracek, Mick Cassidy, Lee Doran, Rob Draper, Ben Harrison, Jordan James, Mike Morrison, Paul Noone, Gareth Price, Adam Sidlow, Aaron Summers, Oliver Wilkes
Loose Forward	Bob Beswick, Dayne Donoghue

They were later to be joined by Wakefield Prop Forward Danny Lima, and Doncaster Scrum Half Joel Penny on permanent deals, while utility Forward Joel Tomkins came in on loan from Wigan.

LEADING FROM THE FRONT

Following the retirement of skipper Terry O'Connor the Vikings needed a new captain for 2007.

When the players reported back for pre-season training coach Steve McCormack intimated that there were several natural leaders and outstanding candidates within the squad for this important role. Ultimately McCormack appointed Mark Smith as captain for the 2007 season, and on receiving the news fans' favourite Smith was reported as being overjoyed with his new role.

"Steve said he thought I would be expecting it but that couldn't be further from the truth." said Smith. "There are some experienced players in the squad and it's phenomenal to be chosen to lead the team. I just hope I can maintain my standards from last season and lead the team back into Super League."

McCormack had no hesitation in appointing the 2006 National League 1 Player's Player of the Year as Captain, and explained:

"Mark is a player who not only wants to play in every game but play 80 minutes in every game. He is an inspiration on the pitch and I know that both players and fans look to him to lead the way."

Following the appointment of Smith as the Vikings' captain McCormack confirmed that Bob Beswick would assume the role of vice-captain. Delighted to re-sign for the Vikings and already looking forward to 2007 Beswick added "I enjoy playing at the Halton Stadium and I see next season as being unfinished business". There is no doubt that the squad Steve McCormack is putting together is better than 2006 and I want to be part of the team who takes Widnes back into Super League."

McCormack was happy to give Beswick, another member of the 2006 National League One Dream Team, the vice-captain's role. "Bob is another player who is vital to the team and his commitment to the cause never waivers. Despite playing in several positions last season, both in the backs and forwards, he never let the team down and, in partnership with Mark

Smith, I believe that in 2007 we will have two outstanding leaders on the pitch."

The justification of the coach's confidence in his Captain and Vice-captain was there for all to see once the season got under way as Smith, the fans' selection as skipper by a country mile, and his lieutenant Beswick set an example followed by the whole squad. On those occasions when skill levels alone were not enough, and results had to be ground out, the team spirit which they engendered was the foundation of several match-winning performances throughout the season.

NEW FOR 2007

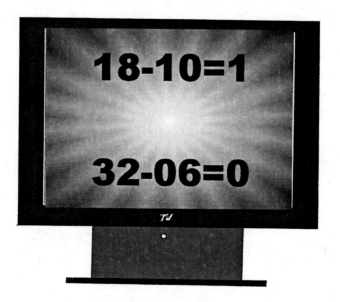

TV coverage for National Leagues

Following rumour and speculation it was finally confirmed on February 1st that the RFL had reached agreement with Sky Sports to broadcast live National League Rugby for the next two years. This would feature NL1 and NL2 matches including the Play-off series, Grand Finals and the Northern Rail Cup Final. It was also confirmed that Widnes Vikings' derby clash with Leigh Centurions would kick off the new National League coverage on Thursday 5th April. Apart from the opening fixture the Vikings were scheduled to feature on four further occasions before the middle of August – the home game

CHAPTER THREE

Kick Off

As preparations for the new season gained momentum, on and off the pitch, the Vikings' Supporters Club, under the guidance of Alan Rae and his committee, held its annual 'Squad Night' in the Bridge Suite at the Halton Stadium on Tuesday 6th February 2007. Hosted by Wire FM's Mark Naughton and Gary McGrath of Radio Merseyside, this enjoyable evening saw Steve McCormack and his first team squad mix happily with an audience of keen and attentive fans just days before the opening fixture in South Wales.

The coach and players were introduced individually to the audience by Mark and Gary, each discussing their hopes and expectations for the forthcoming season. The audience was also treated to some amusing anecdotes about life behind the scenes at the Halton Stadium, with Adam Bowman seemingly the fall-guy of most of the 'in-jokes'!

It was evident that from McCormack down, there was already a very strong team spirit in place, and a united dressing room that was determined to do everything in their individual and collective power to achieve success in 2007.

When the fixtures for the group stages of the Northern Rail

Cup were published Widnes were given an awkward looking trip to Celtic Crusaders, the RFL's latest 'cause celebre'. As the opening day of the 2007 season approached this potential 'banana skin' became an even more uncomfortable proposition as the forecast of heavy snow in South Wales would make playing conditions a great leveller. There had also been concern all week about the snow actually forcing a postponement of this Northern Rail Cup Group 6 match at the Crusaders' Brewery Field ground in Bridgend. However, as the Vikings' squad prepared to leave the Halton Stadium on Thursday Celtic Crusaders' officials remained confident that Friday evening's clash would beat the weather.

Steve McCormack had planned a training session for Thursday morning prior to heading south, but ironically this had to be cancelled due to the weather! Fortunately help was at hand from Billy McGinty the former Widnes Tigers player, now on the coaching staff at Worcester Warriors, who stepped in to offer the use of Worcester's indoor training facilities. McCormack's squad were only too happy to take advantage of this generous offer, with an afternoon training session, before continuing their journey to South Wales, but this wasn't the end of the disruption. On Friday morning the snow closed in on the team's Swansea Hotel and at lunchtime the decision was taken to transfer to a hotel in Port Talbot for their pre-match meal and preparations, and to ensure that they reached the stadium without further incident or delay.

Although there was actually no snow at the ground, heavy falls in the valleys meant that many local fans were unable to get into Bridgend, resulting in a disappointing attendance.

Kick Off

9th February 2007 - NRC Group 6

Celtic Crusaders   6
Widnes Vikings   56

It had been a harrowing day of travelling for both players and fans but, in a portent of what was to come throughout the season, the Vikings produced a performance of stout defence and excellent attacking play as they dominated their opponents in South Wales. After a quiet opening it came as a relief when the breakthrough was finally made in the 18th minute when the club's record points scorer Mick Nanyn converted his own try. Widnes took a firmer grip on proceedings when, eight minutes later, debutant Scott Grix ran through the home defence after taking a clever pass from Mark Smith. Bob Beswick was the next name on the scoresheet with an excellent individual effort, and with Nanyn converting both scores the Vikings held an 18 - 0 lead at half-time.

After the beak the Vikings demonstrated the professionalism that was to become their trademark for the rest of the campaign by adding a further 38 points with a single response from their hosts.

Dennis Moran was the first to cross the line, five minutes into the second period, when he was first to react when his grubber rebounded off a defender, followed four minutes later by Smith who had capitalised on a break from dummy-half by Damien Blanch. The host's response came mid-way through the half, but this only served to spur the Vikings to add further tries through Grix (2), Moran, Blanch, and another debutant, Toa Kohe-Love. Nanyn added a further 5 goals to take his opening day tally to 20 points in an emphatic victory.

After the game Steve McCormack was full of praise for his side, "We prepared well yesterday and despite the change in our plans today the players gave a fully professional performance".

One 'lucky' Widnes supporter having arrived only 2 minutes before the end of the match asked one of players near the dug-out if it had been a good game. The fan was then approached by Steve McCormack who asked him to wait for a couple of minutes after the game. Steve re-appeared to thank the fan for his efforts in getting to the match and promptly gave him his own copy of the match DVD, later adding "I am full of admiration for the way the fans have battled down here today and they deserve so much credit. With the Lady Vikings helping with the costs of last night's accommodation and the players also making a significant contribution, it shows that everyone is working together and has the same goals."

Another anecdote concerns the coach organised by the Supporters Club. The organisers were inadvertently given an incorrect post-code for the stadium and arrived at the Celtic Colliery! Fortunately they were able to find the correct post-code, punch it into the 'Sat-Nav' and arrive in good time for the match!

Others battling against the weather and traffic were not so lucky, with various reports of journeys of up to 11 hours, only to arrive late, or miss the whole game thanks to being gridlocked on the A449 for several hours!

Crusaders:	Duggan, Johnston, Dalle Cort , Blackwood, Ballard, Young, Van Dijk, Cale, Budworth, Dean,Wyatt, Mapp, Quinn. Subs: Toshack, Fitzgerald, I'Anson, Davies
Tries:	Johnston
Goal:	Quinn

Vikings:	Grix, Blanch, Kohe-Love, Nanyn, Dodd, Moran, Kain, Cassidy, Smith, Bracek, Doran, Noone, Beswick. Subs: Webster, Wilkes, James, Harrison.
Tries:	Nanyn, Grix 3, Beswick, Moran 2, Smith, Kohe-Love, Blanch
Goals:	Nanyn (8)
Referee:	Ian Smith Att: 452

18ᵗʰ February 2007 - NRC Group 6

Widnes Vikings	**34**
Leigh Centurions	**20**

This was seen by many as the 'acid test' of Steve McCormack's recruitment and preparations for the 2007 season ahead. The Centurions had been very much a bogey team of Widnes in recent seasons, with the Vikings on the receiving end in some high-scoring matches. Last week's fear of snow had disappeared but there was still an icy anticipation amongst the local supporters as we made our way to the opening fixture at the Halton Stadium and the familiar match-day routine soon kicked in:

Find a parking space – check; have the right change for the Programme and Golden Gamble – check; find your regular seats empty – check; So far so good, everything is reassuringly familiar. The players come out to begin their warm-up to cheers from the faithful who have taken their seats early. Then the first challenge of the new season – identify the new players and fix their numbers in your mind for future reference; but then you remember that there are no Squad Numbers in National League rugby! Oh well I'll have it sussed by October! Thankfully the familiar voice of Announcer Roy Basnett was there to help us through it all. There was just time for a quick glance at the programme and spot that we also had a new face as referee. The 'man in the middle' was an Australian flown over to officiate in the World Club Championship match between St Helens and Brisbane Broncos, and one can only assume that this unusual appointment was to enable Mr Clarke to become familiar with the English winter. To the fans' subsequent dismay this 'international' referee was equally as ineffective at dealing with the visitor's spoiling tactics as others entrusted with the whistle in recent times.

Finally the match was under way and there was more familiarity after just 10 minutes – Widnes 0, Leigh 12. To make matters worse it was ex-Viking Martin Ainscough who was first to react to a kick through the home defence to open the scoring for the visitors.

The groans were deafening, but by half-time Widnes had fought back and began to give an insight into the 2007 vintage of the Vikings. They fought and battled, with no little skill, and by half-time they had scored 10 points with no reply from the visitors. After 18 minutes Gavin Dodd was the beneficiary of a Dennis Moran bomb, as possession was regained and the ball passed out wide for the winger to score easily in the corner. As half-time approached Dodd was again the man on the spot as he capitalised on a 60 metre break from Damien Blanch, who then kicked across field for his fellow winger to register his first brace of tries of the new season. With Mick Nanyn converting Dodd's second score the home side went in at half-time with a 12 – 10 deficit.

Losing possession inside their own 20 metre area led to the Vikings going further behind just three minutes into the second half, but once they had levelled through Toa Kohe-Love's converted try on 53 minutes there was only one winner as a resurgent Vikings took control of the match. Next to score was Andy Kain as he picked up the pieces following another Moran bomb, while our own 'Captain Fantastic', Mark Smith, and Andy Bracek – on loan from Warrington – both dived over between the posts, allowing Nanyn to finish the day with five more goals to add to his tally.

Having survived the first test in front of the home support McCormack confirmed that "the goal today was to win the game and to ensure Leigh didn't get a bonus point. I was disappointed with our start but I knew the work we did in the second quarter would stand us in good stead for the second half," adding that Andy Kain himself "wasn't happy with his first 40 minutes but I told him just to relax and play his natural game and his second half display showed that he is a talented player."

Vikings:	Grix, Blanch, Kohe-Love, Nanyn, Dodd, Moran, Kain, Cassidy, Smith, Bracek, Noone, Wilkes, Beswick. Subs: Webster, Doran, James, Harrison
Tries:	Dodd (2), Kohe-Love, Kain, Smith, Bracek
Goals:	Nanyn (5)
Centurions:	Greenwood, Rudd, Stewart, Alstead, Rivett; Ainscough, Heremaia; Stevens, Clough, John Hill, Styles, Grundy, Jonkers; Subs: Butterworth, Speakman, Cookson, Chris Hill.
Tries:	Ainscough, Clough, Rivett, Rudd
Goals:	Heremaia (2)
Referee:	Stephen Clarke (Aus) Att: 4,133

22nd February 2007   **Disciplinary Hearing**

Mark Smith was found to 'have no case to answer' when the RFL reviewed an incident from Sunday's Northern Rail Cup match against Leigh. He had been placed on report by the referee following a tackle on the Centurions' Aaron Heremaia, who, after receiving treatment on the pitch was carried off on a stretcher, to return later and play a full part for the visitors.

25th February 2007 - NRC Group 6

Widnes Vikings	**60**
London Skolars	**10**

As we approached Round 3 of the group stage of the Northern Rail Cup local debate centred on the relative merits of selecting a full-strength team or 'blooding' some of the younger players in Steve McCormack's first team squad. Opinion seemed to be split evenly with those favouring putting out the 'first team' basing their argument on the benefits of continuity and the increased confidence gained by registering a convincing victory, albeit it against 'lesser' opposition , and an extended winning run. It has to said that the counter-argument carries equal weight in that the experience gained by so-called 'fringe players' at this stage of the season may have proven vital should they have been needed at the 'business end' of the season.

We cannot be sure what McCormack would have done given a completely free choice from his squad, but minor injuries to Damien Blanch, Dennis Moran and Mick Cassidy enabled the coach to give debuts to Dean Gaskell, Andy Kirk and Gareth Price. Whilst rotating the squad the coach also gave seasonal debuts to Darryl Cardiss, and Academy products Adam Bowman and Rob Draper.

There was a disappointingly small 'gate' due in part to a lack of travelling support for the visitors, and the feeling amongst locals that this was not going to be much more than a training run-out. So the match kicked-off in a somewhat eerie atmosphere, with an early score from the Londoners hardly seeming out of place or surprising. The team took this more in their stride than did many of the paying public. As so often happens in cup football the underdog causes an early shock, and maybe this was the jolt Widnes needed against their Division 2 opponents, as they then proceeded to rack up an unanswered 40 points by half-time with Toa Kohe-Love leading the way with four tries, and Rob Draper scoring his first senior try for the Vikings. Unfortunately for the 19 year-old Draper this major milestone was credited over the public address system to Gareth Price!

The second half started quietly and the patience of Vikings fans was tested again as the first score of the second period also went to the visitors, on 50 minutes. However, Mark Smith crossed on the hour with the first of four home tries in ten minutes, which included first tries in Widnes colours for both Kirk and Lee Doran. With Nanyn and Dodd contributing a total of eight goals between them the match petered out with a comfortable 50 point winning margin. The final action of the afternoon was the dismissal of Oliver Wilkes for retaliation following an incident in a tackle with the Skolars' Louw, who was also shown the red card.

Vikings: Dodd, Kirk, Kohe-Love, Nanyn, Gaskell, Grix, Kain, James, Smith, Harrison, Doran, Wilkes, Beswick. Subs: Bowman, Cardiss, Draper, Price

Tries:	Kohe-Love (4), Grix (2), Nanyn, Draper, Smith, Kirk, Doran
Goals:	Nanyn (6), Dodd (2)

Skolars:	Hodgkinson, Williams, Sipthorp, Tozer, Aggrey, Reid, Thorman, Barker, Pittman, Benson, Bell, Maitua, Coleman. Subs: Honor, Castle, Louw, Ellison
Tries:	Maitua, Ellison
Goals:	Thorman

Referee:	Matthew Thomasson	Att: 2,760

4th March 2007 - NRC Group 6

Leigh Centurions	24
Widnes Vikings	8

With the Centurions having surprisingly lost at home to Celtic Crusaders in the last round many Vikings fans were looking forward to the return fixture at Hilton Park, but this was tempered by the news coming out of the Halton Stadium during the week that Damien Blanch, Dennis Moran and Mick Nanyn would not be fit for this game. It had been hoped that their injuries would have cleared up in time, but coach Steve McCormack expressed his confidence in their replacements, and the squad as a whole, prior to this important fixture. Scott Grix made his first return to Leigh since leaving the Centurions for the Vikings having been named Northern Rail Cup Player of the Month by Rugby League World Magazine. Unfortunately it was not to be a happy return for Grix, or his former Leigh team-mate Dean Gaskell, as the Vikings produced a tepid display against a team that seemed, again, to have the Indian Sign over their visitors.

What was to become, to say the least, a physical confrontation kicked off at a wet and windy Hilton Park and Widnes found themselves six points adrift within the first minute, and so for the third match in a row Widnes were chasing the game from the outset. For the next fifteen minutes or so the Vikings carried the fight to Leigh but despite continued possession in good areas they were unable to convert this into points, and the home side capitalised on this with two further tries to lead 16 – 0 at the break.

Worse was to come as the Centurions crossed again in the first minute of the second period, leaving the visitors with the immediate target of at least salvaging a bonus point. Darryl Cardiss eventually made the break-through with an unconverted try in the corner following good work from Kohe-Love, Grix and Andy Kain. As the Vikings fought to further reduce the arrears Dodd made a 40 metre break on 65 minutes, but an ugly incident erupted behind the play, as a Leigh player threw a punch at Andy Bracek, and Mark Smith's arms were held by two opponents whilst a third was punching him! Players from both sides joined the melee, while some tried to calm things down, with the referee eventually showing the yellow card to Rowley of Leigh and Vikings' Gareth Price. The incident was placed 'on report' whilst the match re-started with a penalty to the Vikings. Despite further Widnes pressure the only improvement to the score was another unconverted try, by vice-captain Bob Beswick, but the visitors were denied a bonus point by a further late try from the hosts.

As the travelling supporters made their way home, soaked to the skin from an afternoon on the open terraces, there were two main topics of conversation. Firstly the excessive treatment meted out to Smith, in what seemed to be direct retribution for his 'perceived offence' against Heremaia in the match at the Halton Stadium two weeks previously (for which the RFL determined that he had "no case to answer"), and secondly the inability to start a match 'on the front foot'. Despite Steve McCormack's claims to be "pleased that we created chances" he must have shared the fans' concerns that his players were again caught cold at the start of each half.

Whilst the return of key players from injury would go some way to meeting these concerns, it seemed that addressing the apparent lack of a positive attitude from the first whistle was the coach's biggest problem.

Centurions:	Greenwood, Alstead, Grundy, Stewart, Rivett, Ainscough, Heremaia, Stevens, Rowley, J Hill, Styles, Roberts, Jonkers. Subs: Butterworth, Kay, C Hill, Cookson
Tries:	Roberts, Greenwood, Grundy, Rivett, Cookson
Goals:	Heremaia (2)
Vikings	Dodd, Cardiss, Kohe-Love, Kirk, Gaskell, Grix, Kain, Cassidy, Smith, Bracek, Doran, Noone, Beswick. Subs: Bowman, Wilkes, James, Price
Tries:	Cardiss, Beswick
Referee:	Jamie Leahy Att: 2,291

6th March 2007   **Disciplinary Hearing**

Ollie Wilkes, found guilty of retaliation against an opponent in the recent match against London Skolars, was fined £100 but not suspended following his appearance before a disciplinary hearing at Red Hall. The full adjudication issued by the RFL was:

> Having watched the DVD carefully, it was obvious that player Wilkes took an elbow and went to retaliate in a 'clout for clout' situation. Player Wilkes went down in the tackle to 'give him one back'. The match official was correct to dismiss player Wilkes from the field. Taking into account the circumstances, the Committee felt that a fine of £100 was appropriate and no suspension. The Committee warned player Wilkes that he needed to allow the match officials to deal with these matters on the pitch and not himself.

Speaking after the hearing Vikings' Head Coach Steve McCormack said, "Oliver had a fair hearing and I have no complaints about the outcome," adding that "Oliver did retaliate and the panel dealt with the matter accordingly."

11th March 2007 - CCC 3rd Round

Widnes Vikings	78
Normanton Knights	10

Discussions in the pubs and clubs of Widnes paid little heed to this opening fixture in the Challenge Cup, which following a sponsorship deal with the Rugby Football League, now carries the name of 'Carnegie' in its official title. The main topic of conversation was the treatment meted out to the Widnes players in last weeks Northern Rail Cup match at Leigh; and in particular the apparent barbaric attack on Mark Smith. 'Messageboards' were awash with apparent eye-witness accounts from those who attended the game, many of whom claimed to be within blood-spattering distance of the action. Later in the week it was announced that the RFL had called Mark Smith and Gareth Price to a hearing at Red Hall together with four members of the Leigh team.

Unfortunately the theme of violence was to raise its head again before the end of this match, and again dominate discussions and 'message boards'. It was unfortunate that the day was spoilt by a large proportion of the visiting fans, sat amidst the Widnes supporters in the North Stand, hell-bent on abusive and anti-social behaviour throughout the afternoon. As this alcohol-fuelled behaviour escalated, scuffles broke out between the Normanton fans and stadium stewards, with some fans entering the field of play. With only two minutes left on the clock referee Ian Smith dismissed an apparent plea from stewards to take the players off, and calmly ushered the players through the remaining passage of play.

As far as the on-field action was concerned Steve McCormack had opted to give Ian Webster his first start, in the unfamiliar role of scrum-half, and the former Saints youngster repaid his coach with two tries in a promising debut. It has to be said, however, that despite the impressive scoreline, the game itself was a largely uneventful and one-sided affair, but for the first time since the opening game of the season the Vikings scored first, as Dean Gaskell followed up Paul Noone's grubber to collect his first try for the club in the opening minute. The excitement was tempered in the sixth minute when Scott Grix went to ground and lay motionless for several minutes before being stretchered off with what appeared to be a serious ankle injury. Daryl Cardiss came off the bench to seamlessly slot into the fullback position. Three minutes after the resumption Ollie Wilkes powered over to start a steady stream of tries, including Paul Noone's first try for his home-town club, as the Vikings easily racked up 44 unanswered points by half-time.

In front of a disappointing crowd of only 1,606 Widnes had added a further four tries by the hour mark, with Dennis Moran notching his fourth try of the afternoon with only nine minutes to go. With Gaskell getting his second, and Andy Kirk and Mark Smith joining in the try-fest with a brace each, the fourteen tries had been shared among seven players. As the home side naturally took their foot off the gas the combination of some good attacking play by the Knights and sloppy defence by the Vikings allowed the visitors to cross for two late tries. This was some reward for a team that had been thoroughly out-played, at a canter, by their professional hosts, but had remained 'honest' throughout, not resorting to foul play or spoiling tactics.

Vikings:	Grix, Blanch, Kirk, Nanyn, Gaskell, Moran, Webster, James, Smith, Price, Noone, Wilkes, Beswick. Subs: Cardiss, Draper, Cassidy, Doran
Tries:	Gaskell (2), Wilkes, Noone, Webster (2), Smith (2), Kirk (2), Moran (4)
Goals:	Nanyn (11)
Knights:	Butterfield, Bateman, Hurst, Lewis, Greaves, Atkinson, Hill, Newsome, Woolford, Waterton, Statham, Tilford, Aspinall. Subs: Dobson, Webster, Smith, Barrett
Tries:	Greaves, Hill
Goal:	Hill
Referee:	Ian Smith Att: 1,606

13th March 2007   **Disciplinary Hearing**

Following the fiery encounter against Leigh at Hilton Park six players had been summoned to appear before the RFL's Disciplinary Panel at Red Hall – the Vikings' Mark Smith and Gareth Price were joined by four members of the Centurions team. There was a mixed outcome for the Vikings as Smith was found not guilty of punching, whilst Price received a three match ban and a fine of £150 having been found guilty of running in and punching an opponent.

The adjudication in relation to Mark Smith stated that:

> The Committee were satisfied that you were close to the incident that started the resulting brawl but did not appear to be involved in that. The DVD breaks and you are next shown throwing punches in response to being attacked by three opponents. There is no evidence of you punching before that. Therefore, the Committee were satisfied that you did not throw punches other than to defend yourself against three opponents. The Committee therefore felt that player Smith should be found not guilty.

The judgement on Gareth Price determined that:

> The Committee found player Price guilty of getting involved in an incident which did not concern him. Player Price went for player Rowley and dragged him off. Player Price then attacked his opponent whilst he is on the ground, striking him several times. The Committee felt that player Price was guilty as described by the Match Review Panel. The Committee gave you credit for your admission and noted player Price's poor disciplinary record. This

was an unsavoury incident, it was aggravated and a bad incident which prolonged the brawl. The Committee felt that a three match suspension and a fine of £150 were appropriate.

In reaching its decision the Disciplinary Committee also felt it necessary to add:

There is clearly bad blood between the teams and possibly the clubs. If this is the case, this must be dealt with in a professional manner. The Committee warned the club that future matches involving both clubs would be scrutinised carefully

Three of the Leigh players were found guilty of punching, received fines of £150 each and total bans of ten matches! A fourth player was found not guilty.

18ᵗʰ March 2007 - NRC Group 6

| **London Skolars** | **0** |
| **Widnes Vikings** | **66** |

After last week's outing in the Carnegie Challenge Cup the Vikings journeyed to the capital to resume their Northern Rail Cup campaign against the 'Skolars', and ran in twelve tries in a one-sided encounter, as they secured qualification for the knock-out stages with a match to spare.

With a large contingent from Widnes boosting an otherwise paltry attendance the Vikings kicked off with a strong wind at their backs and wasted no time in taking the lead. In effect the match was won after just 12 minutes as the visitors raced into an 18 – 0 lead, thanks in part to an unlikely 'double' from Ollie Wilkes. Wilkes had scored his first try with only five minutes on the clock before Dennis Moran scored tries either side of Wilkes second effort, with Ian Webster joining in the fun to register a hat-trick in the ten minutes before half-time to give the visitors a 42 – 0 lead at the break.

Toa Kohe-Love ran in the Vikings eighth try just three minutes into the second half, with Mick Nanyn adding a further try, in the 51st minute, to his seven goals in his 200th career appearance. Paul Noone took over the kicking duties to convert another try from Kohe-Love before Andy Kirk touched down with five minutes remaining. As the Vikings continued to attack until the final whistle Moran completed his hat-trick in the last minute, with Noone adding his second goal to complete the scoring. To add to Nanyn's mark, on a day of records, Academy product Mike Morrison, made his debut from the substitute's bench whilst Kohe-Love and Moran reached career totals of 500 and 700 points respectively. In achieving this milestone Moran also passed the 100 point mark for Widnes.

After the match Steve McCormack paid tribute to the professional approach from his squad in such bad conditions, and the promising displays from youngsters Adam Sidlow and Morrison. "Overall we're glad to get through with one game to go. The players performed professionally in bad conditions and it was pleasing to see both Adam Sidlow and Mike Morrison have good games," commented the Vikings coach.

Skolars:	Hodgkinson, Simms, Green, Price, Webster (W), Nowland, Thorman, Louw, Pittman, Ellison, Brown, Maitua, Coleman. Subs: Reid, Shears, Miller, Barker

Vikings:	Grix, Kirk, Kohe-Love, Nanyn, Gaskell, Moran, Webster (I), James, Smith, Wilkes, Doran, Noone, Beswick. Subs: Cardiss, Sidlow, Morrison, Dodd
Tries:	Wilkes (2), Moran (3), Webster (3), Kohe-Love (2), Nanyn, Kirk
Goals:	Nanyn (7), Noone (2)

Referee:	Ashley Klein	Att: 789

25th March 2007 - NRC Group 6

Widnes Vikings	**32**
Celtic Crusaders	**10**

With several key players – Toa Kohe-Love, Mick Nanyn, Dennis Moran, Mark Smith, Mick Cassidy and Gareth Price - missing through injury, suspension or squad rotation, and Dean Gaskell dropped to the bench, it was an unfamiliar line-up which took the field. Unfortunately on the evidence of the first half play their replacements were as unfamiliar to each other as they were to those sitting in the stands. With the creative king-pins of Smith and Moran absent, and recent live-wire scrum-half Ian Webster going off after seven minutes with an ankle injury, there was a conspicuous lack of cohesive movement around the park.

During a turgid first 40 minutes a defensively well-organised Crusaders easily held their hosts at bay and took the lead themselves on eight minutes. Duggan, their outstanding player crossed for the first of his brace of tries, whilst the Vikings were down to twelve men while Webster's replacement was preparing to enter the fray. Slowly the home side edged back into the game and eventually, after Jordan James had a try ruled out by the touch judge, Adam Bowman scored in the corner following a long ball from Ollie Wilkes. Although the pacy Duggan again extended the visitors lead following a harsh 'knock-on' decision against Darryl Cardiss, Rob Draper powered over the line to reduce the deficit to two points (8 – 10) as the half drew to a close.

Thankfully it was a different Widnes that were welcomed onto the pitch by the Vikings Starlites for the second half with two tries in the space of five minutes from Scott Grix. With Wilkes held up short of the line the Vikings continued to press and Grix grounded the ball to put the home side in front for the first time. His second try came as he attacked the line from acting half-back following a last-ditch tackle on Andy Kirk. Gavin Dodd took over the kicking duties from the absent Nanyn, to convert both tries. On 57 minutes the un-sung Cardiss scored the try of the match when he raced in to finish off a sweeping move of first-time passes involving James, Wilkes and Paul Noone to finish off the men from the valleys. Grix completed his hat-trick with a try which show-cased the turn round in fortunes for the Vikings when he chipped the defence and collected the ball to score with two minutes left on the clock.

As the 'hooter' sounded the small, but vociferous, group of Crusaders supporters were still proudly supporting their team who had certainly run their hosts close, in a match that was interesting rather than entertaining. For the home fans the second half performance and result finally eased some of the frustrations of the first half, and Steve McCormack, whilst critical of the first half display, was rightly pleased with the re-sponse from his players, several of whom were again Academy products, in the second period. "In the first half we failed to lay a platform" said McCormack, "there was no ball control and no enthusiasm. The second half was in sharp contrast and I thought we did well against a Celtic side who came here to win the game."

Vikings:	Grix, Blanch, Kirk, Cardiss, Dodd, Kain, Webster, James, Beswick, Wilkes, Draper, Doran, Noone. Subs: Gaskell, Sidlow, Bowman, Morrison,
Tries:	Bowman, Draper, Grix (3), Cardiss
Goals:	Dodd (4)
Crusaders:	Duggan, Epton, Dalle Cort , Quinn, Johnston, Young, Van Dijk, Cale, Budworth, Dean, Martin, Fitzgerald, Mapp. Subs: Ballard, I'Anson, Cushion, Davies
Tries:	Duggan (2)
Goal:	Quinn

Refreee: David Merrick   Att: 2,540

1ˢᵗ April 2007 - CCC 4ᵗʰ Round

Widnes Vikings	**24**
Wigan Warriors	**34**

Following weeks of anticipation the 'big match' atmosphere finally returned to the Halton Stadium, along with the BBC cameras, as the nation saw the Vikings take on a Wigan team packed with expensive signings and International players. Steve McCormack was without ex-Wigan warhorse Mick

Cassidy and the burgeoning talent of Ian Webster through injury.

A day of drama and no little entertainment began with the BBC's Clare Balding interviewing Referees supremo Stuart Cummings about the RFL's innovative introduction of armchair fans having a 75% input to 'Video Referee' decisions, by 'voting' through their remote control. Clare later reminded viewers of the date as the teams ran out onto the pitch! Meanwhile those of us in the stadium had been treated to live pre-match entertainment from the Lancashire Hotpots, with their rendition of 'Chippy Tea', and the now regular appearance of the Vikings Starlite dancers.

The match kicked off with an atmosphere and attendance not witnessed at the ground since relegation from Super League, with the strong contingent of ex-Wigan players in the Widnes line-up only serving to add an 'edge' to the proceedings. In typical underdog fashion it was the home side that took the fight to their more illustrious visitors, with as if scripted, former Wigan player Dennis Moran at the heart of everything as the Warriors line was kept under early pressure. As a result of this early pressure the Vikings took a sixth minute lead when Damien Blanch, hovering above the touch-line, passed inside to Toa Kohe-Love whose outstretched arm planted the ball over the line as he lost his footing. Minutes later the Vikings nearly extended their lead when man-of-the-match Bob Beswick lost control a split second before touching down under pressure from three Wigan defenders. The joy of the home fans was temporarily quashed as O'Loughlin breached an outstanding defence to level matters on nineteen minutes. However two penalties from Mick Nanyn sent the Vikings in at half-time with a deserved lead of 8 – 4.

As so often happens the half-time break came at the wrong time for the underdog, and while Widnes struggled to find the rhythm and power of the first 40 minutes the Warriors took the lead for the first time as Leuluai scored on 43 minutes, with Richards converting. Following a period of open end-to-end rugby Widnes played their way back into contention, with Scott Grix crossing on the hour to allow the Vikings to edge ahead again by 12 – 10, with the delirious home fans now sensing a possible giant-killing. Unfortunately this finally stirred the visitors into action as they demonstrated their superior passing and movement to add four converted tries in the space of seven minutes, leaving the home fans fearing a rout. But the 2007 vintage of the Vikings did not give in easily and they deservedly narrowed the deficit to just 10 points with two late converted tries by Jordan James and Paul Noone.

Whilst paying tribute to the performance of Bob Beswick, a proud McCormack added that "It was a great team effort" and that "the difference in the end was that Wigan took their chances and we didn't". With regard to the "amazing" atmosphere in the ground the coach said that the players had even commented on it at half-time, and added "Not only have the players set a benchmark for the Co-operative National League season which starts on Thursday but so have the fans. It was a great occasion and on behalf of everybody at the Club I'd like to thank all those who came along and gave their support."

Vikings:	Grix, Blanch, Kohe-Love, Nanyn, Dodd, Moran, Kain, James, Smith, Wilkes, Doran, Noone, Beswick. Subs: Summers, Sidlow, Cardiss, Morrisson.
Tries:	Kohe-Love, Grix, James, Noone
Goals:	Nanyn (4)

Warriors:	Ashton, Calderwood, Bailey, Goulding, Richards, Barrett, Leuluai, Fielden, Higham, Palea'asina, Hock, Fletcher, O'Loughlin. Subs: Millard, Prescott, Hansen, Hill
Tries:	O'Loughlin, Richards (2), Goulding, Barrett, Leuluai
Goals:	Richards (5)
Referee:	Steve Ganson Att: 6,006

5th April 2007   **Chairman quits !**

With anticipation of the 'League' season boosted by the performance against Wigan, Widnes fans were dealt a stunning blow on the morning of the opening fixture when the Widnes Weekly News ran a front page story under a dramatic "Vaughan: I Quit" headline.

Ian Cheveau exclusively broke the story that the then chairman, Stephen Vaughan, had quit on the opening day of the League campaign – the day the Vikings had to negotiate a tricky clash with Leigh Centurions. He had spoken with Steve McCormack the previous evening to inform him that the chairman was going to pull the plug on the financial backing he had pledged, as a result of a backroom dispute with his fellow board members, and quit.

McCormack was obviously shocked, and although the ripples had turned into waves behind the scenes, he prepared himself to work with the third chairman of his short reign.

Rumours hovered over the Club like a storm cloud as we looked forward to the big kick-off, whilst quotes attributed to Mr Vaughan in the local press suggested that he was unhappy with the level of support offered by his fellow Directors. Through his share purchase, and loans Mr Vaughan was thought to have invested more than any previous Director of the Club.

However, by the time kick-off arrived this bombshell seemed to have been put to the back of people's minds as a ground-swell of the 'we will survive' attitude became dominant in conversations and on 'messageboards'. There was an unusual feeling of positivity in the air as though the fans were saying to Mr Vaughan 'we have a strong team, playing well and we will carry on regardless.' This siege mentality seemed to bring the fans closer to club, and there was a feeling that maybe this could be the catalyst for a new bond between club and supporters that would propel us together into Super League.

As if to underline this feeling, Chief Executive Peter Barrow made the following statement:

> The Board held an emergency meeting this afternoon following the departure of Stephen Vaughan from the Board. They wish to thank Stephen for his support and financial input which has kept the Club alive over the past year. They confirm their earlier message of 'business as usual' with the Board, staff and players all totally committed to getting the Club back into Super League.
>
> Pete Barrow
> Chief Executive

Widnes Vikings   **46**
Leigh Centurions   **12**

As a result of negotiations between the RFL and Sky Sports, National League fixtures were, for the first time, added to the list of live transmissions by the satellite broadcaster, and this match was chosen for the initial broadcast. Much debate took place locally about the 6.05pm kick-off on a working day, imposed by Sky as they were already committed to the Bradford v Leeds game kicking off at 8.00pm. Wider indignation was felt among supporters of all National League clubs when it was realised that there would be no 'fee' or 'compensation' paid to participating clubs to offset the obvious drop in attendances at the televised games – unlike Super League!

On the playing front the 17 who did duty against Wigan were rightly included in the squad for this match, supplemented by the return of Gareth Price, Mick Cassidy and Andy Kirk; whilst following the recent incident-ridden fixture at Hilton Park, the hope was that the right attitude would be displayed by all the players on the park.

On a sunny evening excellent pre-match entertainment from the Vikings Starlites and X Factor contestant Shaun Rogerson, who hails from Abram, got the crowd in the mood for the main event. With the home crowd desperate for success against their bitter rivals Mark Smith led his team on to the pitch to a welcome which rivalled that for last week's cup-tie. Within two minutes the Vikings had surged into a six point lead as Mick Nanyn created and converted Scott Grix's opening try, with the hosts doubling their advantage on 15 minutes. Dennis Moran's accurate kick gave Damien Blanch the opportunity to use his pace to out-strip the defence, collect the ball and score, enabling Nanyn to chalk up his 2000th career point with the conversion. A minute after Nanyn's 28th minute penalty had extended the lead Blanch's pace panicked the Leigh defence who coughed up a loose ball. Moran was first to the ball and passed to the supporting Toa Kohe-Love for the kiwi centre to score near the flag. Moran himself scored the final try of the half, in the 38th minute, when his strength allowed him to get between two defenders and extend his arm to score, giving

Nanyn the chance to convert and take the half-time score to 24 - 0. The score reflected the fact that most of the first 40 minutes had been played in the visitors half, with Widnes alert to every loose ball and equally dominant in attack and defence.

With Moran at the centre of almost every move from the Vikings they continued to dominate their opponents in the second half, adding a further four tries, the first coming from a weaving run from Gavin Dodd on 44 minutes. Grix and Dodd then created the space for Moran to cross on 60 minutes, with the Leigh defence torn to shreds, whilst four minutes later Grix sold the Leigh defence an outrageous dummy to score by the posts, with Nanyn's conversions making the score 40 − 0. As the players seemed to tire from their exertions against Wigan the previous week Leigh scored two tries in the last ten minutes which disguised the fact that they had been totally outplayed. Former Widnes favourite (and villain in some people's eyes) Adam Hughes converted both of the tries from scrum-half Aaron Heremaia. Sandwiched between these two efforts was a typical poacher's effort from Moran as he collected a loose ball and sprinted 40 metres to complete his hat-trick and man of the match performance.

The previously camera shy Vikings had put on two top class televised performances in successive weeks, and at a stroke demonstrated their class, power and determination to the rest of National League One, as the players soaked up the tumultuous applause from the stands as the final hooter sounded.

Steve McCormack paid tribute to his side following the victory. "I though the players' skills and fitness levels were superb and it's a tribute to both them and the coaching staff that they performed so well so soon after the Wigan game.

Vikings:	Grix, Blanch, Kohe-Love, Nanyn, Dodd, Moran, Kain, James, Smith, Wilkes, Doran, Noone, Beswick. Subs: Summers, Cassidy, Cardiss, Price.
Tries:	Grix (2), Blanch, Kohe-Love, Moran (3), Dodd
Goals:	Nanyn (7)

Centurions:	Greenwood, Smyth, Alstead, Hughes, Rivett, Ainscough, Heremaia, Stevens, Clough, Wilson, Hill, Grundy, Roberts. Subs: Butterworth, Jonkers, Richardson, Cookson
Tries:	Heremaia (2)
Goals:	Hughes (2)

Referee:	Gareth Hewer.	Att: 3,792.

9th April 2007 - NL1

Rochdale Hornets   **18**
Widnes Vikings   **40**

Another tremendous turn-out by the Vikings travelling support witnessed a hard-fought victory over a Rochdale team smarting from a mauling by Whitehaven in their opening league fixture a few days earlier. With the fans segregated it was plain to see that no more than 250 out of a reported attendance of 1,485 were supporting the home team.

Whilst this was not the same assured Widnes that had performed so well against Wigan and Leigh, it was in the end a workmanlike performance with flashes of creative, attacking rugby, which eventually produced a comfortable victory. After a reasonable opening period, and taking an early lead when Damien Blanch touched down in the corner, the Vikings contrived to hand the initiative to their hosts as they entered a period of mediocrity for much of the first half. Blanch's score only served to prompt a strong fight-back from the Hornets as they raised their game to run in two converted tries to take a 12 – 4 lead. The Vikings countered when, first Dennis Moran gratefully collected a gift ten yards out to score under the posts, and then Mick Nanyn was first to react to a Moran 'grubber' to give the visitors a fortunate 14 - 12 advantage. This did not last for long as the Hornets hit back again as danger man Fagborun raced through a static defence to give the hosts a deserved lead of 18 – 14 at the break.

Rochdale had looked much the sharper side during the first period but Steve McCormack obviously found the right words for his half-time team-talk, as the Vikings were more like their recent selves after the break. After surviving another bright opening to the half by their hosts, who dominated early possession, Widnes scored 26 unanswered points to eventually win their second match of the Easter period with something to spare.

The pendulum finally swung in Widnes' favour as the returning Ian Webster reacted first to a fumbled Moran 'bomb' near the Rochdale line, to begin the Vikings revival. Although Nanyn's conversion allowed the Vikings to edge four points clear, the Vikings' defence still had to work overtime to protect their lead as a series of penalties gave the home side good possession. Having survived this self-inflicted pressure Widnes gained some breathing space when, following a move down the left, Gavin Dodd took Nanyn's smart off-load to touch down in the corner. Nanyn then converted two penalties in quick succession, before completing his hat-trick with two late tries, one of which came as a result of another surging run from the outstanding Paul Noone.

Vikings:	Grix, Blanch, Kohe-Love, Nanyn, Dodd, Moran, Kain, James, Smith, Wilkes, Doran, Noone, Beswick. Subs: Summers, Webster, Kirk, Price.
Tries:	Blanch, Moran, Nanyn (3), Dodd, Webster.
Goals:	Nanyn (6)
Hornets:	Andrews, Johnson, Patterson, King, Fagborun, Svabic, Hasty, Baldwin, McConnell, Smith, Anderson, Blanchard, Goulden. Subs: Corcoran, Norman, Gorski, Ball.
Tries:	King, McConnell, Fagborun.
Goals:	King (3)
Referee:	Craig Halloran Att: 1,485

13th April 2007 - NL1

Sheffield Eagles   4
Widnes Vikings   46

The Vikings travelled to Sheffield for their third match in eight days, to complete the hectic opening period to the National League season. They were backed up by another excellent turn-out of travelling support as fans dashed from work to make the 8.00pm kick-off at the Don Valley Stadium. Open on three sides, the stadium, built for the World Student

Games of 1991, at a cost of £29m, and better known for hosting Athletics meetings, afforded the unlikely view of Sheffield by street light as darkness fell. Whilst the athletics track which surrounds the pitch made the players somewhat isolated the travelling fans yet again made their presence felt, as several of their heroes responded to the fans' chants to 'give us a wave' !

The fans had barely made themselves comfortable in their seats before Bob Beswick charged down an attempted clearance by the Sheffield defence on the final tackle of the first set, to gather the ball and score the Vikings opening try in the first minute. This set the standard for a very one-sided first half in which a totally dominant Widnes team added further tries through Mick Nanyn, Gavin Dodd, Dennis Moran, and skipper Mark Smith, all of which were converted by Nanyn to give the Vikings a half-time lead of 30 – 0. Such was the dominance of the Vikings that the referee seemed to take pity on the hosts when he 'ignored' Ford carrying the ball over the dead ball line, and then returning to the field of play, when fielding a Widnes kick. Both touch judges flagged furiously, only for the referee to dismiss what they, and the entire crowd, had seen!

Expectations were obviously high for a continuation of the rout in the second half, but as often happens, the half-time whistle halted the Widnes steam-roller, and it was not until the final quarter that the lead was increased. The home side had come out after the break, no doubt fired up by their coach, and put on a much stronger performance for twenty minutes, until former Eagles star Jordan James scored under the posts to ignite another surge from the visitors. Tries from Damien Blanch and the impressive Nanyn further extended the lead, until a 78th minute consolation enabled Sheffield to avoid the 'whitewash'.

Whilst the Vikings returned home with their 100% league

record intact following another impressive performance, some fans were concerned by their failure to score more points in the second period. Of more significant concern was the fact that Ian Webster failed to appear for the second half with what appeared to be a further ankle injury.

Coach Steve McCormack, whilst pleased with the result in the context of the games played in the eight day period, was nonetheless "disappointed that we didn't score a few more tries", adding that the players were themselves "disappointed at the way that the second half went".

Eagles: Woodcock, Ford, Bravo, Newlove, Hurst, Lindsay, Brambani, Howieson, Cook, Morton, Brown, Holdstock, Edwards. Subs: Farrow, Corcoran, Trayler, Stringer

Try: Farrow

Vikings: Grix, Blanch, Kohe-Love, Nanyn, Dodd, Moran, Webster, James, Smith, Wilkes, Doran, Noone, Beswick. Subs: Summers, Cassidy, Kirk, Price

Tries: Beswick, Nanyn (2), Dodd, Moran, Smith, James, Blanch

Goals: Nanyn (7)

Referee: Robert Hicks   Att: 1,211

Kick Off

NL1 Table

	P	W	D	L	B	F	A	Diff	Pts
Castleford	3	3	0	0	0	187	38	149	9
Widnes	3	3	0	0	0	132	34	98	9
Whitehaven	3	3	0	0	0	88	28	60	9
Batley	3	1	1	1	0	58	113	-55	5
Leigh	3	1	0	2	1	76	82	-6	4
Halifax	3	1	0	2	1	84	93	-9	4
Dewsbury	3	1	0	2	1	55	76	-21	4
Sheffield	3	0	1	2	1	46	92	-46	3
Doncaster	3	1	0	2	0	46	138	-92	3
Rochdale	3	0	0	3	0	42	120	-78	0

18th April 2007   **Board Statement**

It was announced that the Club's Board of Directors had moved swiftly to ensure the short-term future of the club following the resignation of former chairman Stephen Vaughan. The announcement, designed to allay the fears of the club's supporters and at the same time counter "scurrilous" rumours in the press and circulating within the game, is reproduced below in full:

Following the resignation of Stephen Vaughan the remaining directors have today put in a cash injection of £150,000 which will take care of the Club's short-term financial requirements.

They are also putting into place strategies to ensure the Club's long-term future. These include seeking to ap-

71

point additional directors to the Board and investigating additional funding opportunities; the Club has no bank borrowing or Crown Creditor obligations.

The Club is disappointed with the scurrilous rumours, in which there is no foundation, that have appeared in the media and are currently circulating within the game.

It is also disappointed that individual players have been approached by other Clubs and intends to investigate these illegal approaches and submit its findings to the Rugby Football League.

Everybody at the Club is determined to ensure that Widnes Vikings continues its excellent start to the season, beginning with Sunday's Northern Rail Cup Tie with Batley Bulldogs.

Pete Barrow
Chief Executive

At the same time fans were expressing great concern that a certain part of the local media was concentrating on dramatic, but negative stories – which were later proved to be unfounded – rather than upbeat reports on the club's 100% start to the league campaign.

19th April 2007   **New signing**

While the local press ran stories of the Club's impending demise it was announced, with immaculate timing, that Wakefield Trinity prop Danny Lima had agreed terms to join the

Vikings for the remainder of the season. The former War-rington Prop forward had a loan spell with Salford City Reds in 2006 prior to moving to Belle Vue for 2007, having rep-resented Sydney Roosters, Canberra Raiders and Manly Sea Eagles in Australia. Lima immediately started training with his new club, but was not available for selection until a protracted application to have his work permit transferred from Wake-field to Widnes was finalised on 21st May. Whilst fans were as ever divided on the merits of this addition to the squad, one thing was agreed – it was not the action of a Club preparing to go to the wall!

22nd April 2007 - NRC- KO1

Widnes Vikings	62
Batley Bulldogs	6

Steve McCormack's declaration that his intention was to win this competition came one step closer as his charges qualified for the quarter-finals, following this ultimately easy victory over the Bulldogs. The Vikings struggled through a turgid opening twenty minutes as the physical and delaying tactics of the visitors prevented the hosts from imposing their open style on the game. During this period Toa Kohe-Love was placed on report following an incident where Ollie Wilkes was head-butted by an opponent.

The deadlock was eventually broken by Andy Kain, who, whilst his legions of detractors were imploring him to pass, jinked past a group of defenders to touch down near the posts. With Mick Nanyn having to sit this one out through illness Gavin Dodd assumed the kicking responsibilities and added the extras. The score was nearly doubled straight from the kick-off as Grix was just beaten to a kick from Andy Kirk by the boot of a defender. Having gained the upper hand Mark Smith created a gap for Mick Cassidy to score, while minutes later Dean Gaskell out-jumped a defender to claim a bomb from Kain to touch down in the corner. Kain then collected an off-load from Bob Beswick to score his second try, while Dennis Moran began the move which eventually allowed him to gather Gaskell's kick to score, and the Vikings went in at half-time with a 28 – 0 lead.

Four minutes into the second half Smith scored what will be the easiest try of his career. Moran kicked into the 'in-goal' area and the lone Batley defender completely missed his attempted clearance while the attendant Smith simply turned, bent down, and placed his hand on the ball. Suddenly the lead surged to 52 – 0 as Smith's creative abilities engineered openings for Bob Beswick and Wilkes, whilst a flowing passing movement from the left ended with Damien Blanch putting Gaskell through on the right wing, for his second try of the game. Dodd continued an excellent afternoon's work with the boot.

Slack defensive work allowed Batley to score a consolation try, but the Vikings responded to this impertinence with Paul Noone and Kirk adding further tries as they ran out easy winners to claim a place in the next round. Having turned the poor performance of the opening quarter into one of total dominance there was even time for the PA announcer to inform us, during a break in play, that it was Noone's birthday, which prompted the North Stand to burst into a spontaneous rendition of 'Happy Birthday' !

By the time that supporters had downed their first post-match pint it was known that our reward was to be a return visit to Spotland to take on the Hornets in the quarter-final. Due to planned maintenance work on their pitch, shared with Rochdale FC, Widnes gained the benefit of home advantage when the fixture was subsequently switched to the Halton Stadium.

Vikings:	Grix, Gaskell, Kohe-Love, Kirk, Dodd, Moran, Kain, James, Smith, Wilkes, Doran, Noone, Beswick. Subs: Summers, Cassidy, Blanch, Price
Tries:	Kain (2), Cassidy, Gaskell (2), Moran, Smith, Beswick, Wilkes, Noone, Kirk
Goals:	Dodd (9)
Bulldogs:	Lingard: Lindsay, Mossop, Langley, Marns, Gordon, Barlow, Rourke, Lythe,Best, Cooke, Spears, Farrell Subs: Rourke, Menzies, McLoughlin, Simpson
Try:	Lythe
Goal:	Gordon
Referee:	Peter Taberner. Att: 2,140

26th April 2007 - NL1

Widnes Vikings	**48**
Halifax	**12**

Chosen again for 'live' TV coverage by Sky meant that the Vikings had only four days to recover from the bruising Northern Rail Cup encounter with Batley. However they managed to start the game on the front foot with Mick Nanyn taking a crisp pass from Bob Beswick to score in the corner barely two minutes into the game. Unable to build on this early lead the Vikings struggled to establish any form of dominance and after thirty minutes found themselves trailing 12 – 4 largely due to the creative skills of former Viking Ian Watson. As the interval approached the home side had added some continuity to their play and began a run of 44 un-answered points when Toa Kohe-Love off-loaded to put Scott Grix in under the posts. Nanyn added the conversion before adding a penalty on the 'hooter' for Widnes to go in all square at the interval.

Speculation that Steve McCormack would be 'burning the paint off the dressing room walls' at half-time seemed close to the mark as Widnes roared into the second period and soon established control of the game as captain Mark Smith crashed over the line in the 43rd minute. Nanyn followed his skipper over the try line four minutes later, with the lead soon being further extended as the Halifax fullback completely misjudged a Beswick 'bomb' to leave the chasing Dennis Moran the simple task of dropping, unchallenged, on the ball to secure a further four points.

In the 63rd minute Grix and Beswick broke from defence with such speed that they left their support struggling in their wake, and it seemed that an opportunity had been lost as the ball carrier was smothered in the tackle. From the resultant play-the-ball, deep in Halifax territory, a quick passing movement saw the ball move across the pitch from the left wing for Kohe-Love to cut in from the right to score, with the Halifax defence split wide open, to establish a 34 – 12 lead. The next score owed everything to the speed and agility of the flying Damien Blanch as he left the Hornets' defence for dead in centre-field and sprinted 70 metres for the most eye-catching try of the night. It was fitting, however, that points-machine Nanyn produced an impressive change of pace to sprint over the line from some 30 metres out to complete his hat-trick, before Jordan James scored the final try with a couple of minutes remaining. Forty-four unanswered points had not only clinched the match, and restored confidence, but took the Vikings back to the top of NL1, if only for a few days.

Afterwards McCormack declared that he was pleased with his side's efforts, praising the first-half defensive effort, and adding that "the attitude of the players was superb and they got their rewards in the second period."

Vikings:	Grix, Blanch, Kohe-Love, Nanyn, Dodd, Moran, Webster, James, Smith, Wilkes,Doran, Noone, Beswick. Subs: Summers, Cassidy, Kirk, Price
Tries:	Nanyn (3), Grix, Smith, Moran, Kohe-Love, Blanch, James
Goals:	Nanyn (6)
Halifax:	White, Gibson, Roberts, Varkulis, Greenwood, Hartley, Watson, Southern, Penkywicz, Watene, Larder, Smith, Joseph. Subs: Jones, Ball, Trinder, Wrench
Tries:	Gibson (2)
Goals:	Hartley (2)
Referee:	Robert Hicks Att: 3,042

1st May 2007   **Disciplinary Hearing**

Toa Kohe-Love, placed on report for an incident in the Northern Rail Cup game against Batley was banned for a staggering 5 matches and fined £100! Even allowing for the 'rose-tinted' view the general consensus was that this was a harsh penalty, for an impulsive rather than malicious offence, compared to recent punishments meted out to players from other clubs guilty of prolonged and deliberate attacks on opponents.

Kohe-Love was advised by the Committee that:

> Having viewed the DVD and listened to player Kohe Love's explanations, it is apparent that you yourself appreciate the seriousness of this incident. That is no doubt why you took yourself off at half time. Misconduct of this type has the real potential for serious injury. The opponent was not looking at player Kohe Love when you struck him. The Committee noted that player Kohe Love had not been before this Committee since 2001 but taking into account the circumstances of this incident, felt that a five match suspension and a fine of £100 were appropriate.

Whilst the majority of fans seemed truly shocked by the severity of the punishment meted out to a player with a clean disciplinary record for the past six years, the club chose not to appeal against the committees findings, perhaps mindful of further incidents yet to come before the disciplinary panel in the near future.

6th May 2007 - NL1

| Widnes Vikings | 66 |
| Batley Bulldogs | 14 |

As the Bulldogs returned to town a very disappointing attendance of under 3,000 saw the Vikings again struggle to assert any early dominance over their visitors, despite a fifth minute try from Dennis Moran. It was deep into the second quarter before they displayed any measure of superiority in a match which bore a striking resemblance to the Northern Rail Cup match two weeks previously. With much of the match played in a steady drizzle an early portent of what was to come was a rare knock-on by Scott Grix which led to the Bulldogs drawing level after eight minutes, and then taking an unlikely lead when a converted penalty gave them an 8 - 6 advantage.

After what seemed an endless sequence of handling errors Paul Noone reacted to a short pass on the angle from Mark Smith to run in from some 10 metres out to put the Vikings back in front on the half-hour. This heralded a period of 30 minutes during which the hosts scored 48 points. Gavin Dodd was next to score when he was first to react to a kick through from Grix, and Grix himself then dodged several tackles to score by the posts. On the stroke of half-time Moran sprinted in from 30 metres after a Batley player knocked-on while attempting to intercept another pass from the resurgent Grix.

Although the early play did nothing to build confidence in the stands this was yet another display of character and teamwork from Widnes. Nothing exemplified this more than the sight of Damien Blanch following a kick from Smith, sprinting down his wing from half-way to tackle a Batley player in his in-goal area to earn a repeat set.

After the re-start Nanyn was put in by a short pass from Bob Beswick to score an early try before Blanch made a trademark break down the centre, from deep in his half, but with the last man at his mercy he chose to slow down and wait for the supporting Andy Kirk to take a short pass 20 metres out and score under the posts. The Bulldogs continued to show glimpses of incisive rugby and added a further try on fifty-six minutes, but the Vikings responded immediately as first Ollie Wilkes crashed over, and then Smith brought up the fifty point mark with just over an hour played. In the closing period Grix stretched for the line as he was tackled to grab his

Dreams To Reality

fourteenth try of the season, and fittingly Moran concluded the scoring by intercepting a pass on his own 10 metre line and sprinted the length of the pitch to complete his fourth hat-trick of the season with the Batley defence trailing in his wake. Mick Nanyn completed an excellent afternoon's work with his eleventh conversion from eleven attempts.

Steve McCormack commented: "The first 20 minutes were disappointing as we failed to hold the ball. You can't blame the conditions because they didn't worry Batley. However once the likes of Mark Smith, Paul Noone and Dennis Moran took the game by the scruff of the neck it was a much better display."

Vikings:	Grix: Blanch, Kirk, Nanyn, Dodd, Moran, Webster, James, Smith, Wilkes, Doran, Noone, Beswick. Subs: Summers, Cassidy, Gaskell, Price.
Tries:	Moran(3), Noone, Dodd, Grix (2), Nanyn, Kirk, Wilkes, Smith
Goals:	Nanyn (11)
Bulldogs:	Lingard: Lindsay, Laurie, Langley, Marns, Gallagher, Duffy, Stenchion, Lythe, McLoughlin, Henderson, Spears, P Farrell Subs: Patterson, C Farrell, Menzies, Simpson.
Tries:	Lindsay, Farrell
Goals:	Duffy (3)
Referee:	David Merrick Att: 2,753

17ᵗʰ May 2007 - NL1

Castleford Tigers	**20**
Widnes Vikings	**44**

This was a match, thrown up by the sceptics as another 'acid test', that had been anticipated in equal measure by the staunch supporters, and the hyper-critical fans who were waiting to see 'the wheels come off' the Vikings bandwagon. Lose this match and the 'stay-aways' would be only too ready to say 'I told you so'! Both teams went into the match boasting 100% records in the League, but it was the Vikings who were triumphant, against the team many pundits (outside the immediate environs of the Halton Stadium) had installed as favourites to secure promotion back to Super League.

In another match covered by the Sky Sports cameras the Vikings assumed early control when after five minutes Gavin Dodd ran on to Bob Beswick's inch-perfect kick through the Castleford defence, and then, after 11 minutes, Mark Smith capitalised on more good interplay between Beswick and Paul Noone to score under the posts. Mick Nanyn converted Smith's try to give the visitors an early 10 – 0 lead, and they went in at the interval leading 12 – 4 when Nanyn added a 40 metre penalty after a Castleford try had briefly brought them back into contention.

Only ten minutes into the second half the lead was extended when Jordan James was the beneficiary of a short pass from Smith following slick build up play between Noone and Beswick; while four minutes later the lead was further extended to 24 – 4 when Ian Webster followed up a kick by Dennis Moran. Webster was all smiles, as despite appearing to knock on as he grounded the ball, the video referee controversially awarded the try! With twenty minutes left Beswick was again the provider, when receiving an off-load from Dodd his kick dissected the Tigers defence on their 10 metre line for Smith to collect and dive over the line. Minutes later the strong running Andy Kirk took on the home defence before setting up Damien Blanch to score in the corner against his former employers, to bring the score to 32 -4 in Widnes' favour.

Two converted tries from the Tigers – one following a fancy pirouette 10 metres out from Brough - brought the score back to 32 – 16, only for the visitors to display their ability to score at will as first Smith returned the favour to put Beswick in under the posts, and then Blanch gathered a loose ball to race in from the 40 metre line. In each case the boot of Mick Nanyn added the 'extras' to take the score to 44- 16 before the Tigers scored a consolation try on the final whistle.

Despite several outstanding individual performances Steve McCormack paid tribute to a great team effort, backed up by the tremendous travelling support. "The support we receive has been fantastic this year and last night was no exception", added McCormack. "It took a lot of effort for people to travel over 80 miles on a Thursday evening and we were all delighted with the numbers who made the journey. Once again the players commented on how good it was to have such vociferous support. They are enjoying playing at the moment and I know they are enjoying the response from the fans".

On a lighter note McCormack also found time to take some credit for the success of Danny Brough's short kick-offs, as he offered the opinion that "Danny Brough caused us a bit of trouble with his short kick-offs but he was only able to do this because we scored so many tries!"

Tigers: Donlan, Wainwright, Dixon, Shenton, Owen, McGoldrick, Brough, Higgins, Henderson, Glassie, Guttenbeil, Barker, Charles. Subs: Boyle, Saxton, Lupton, Leafa

Tries:	Owen, Donlan (2), Brough
Goals:	Brough (2)

Vikings:	Grix, Blanch, Kirk, Nanyn, Dodd, Moran, Webster, Cassidy, Smith, Wilkes, Doran, Noone, Beswick. Subs: Summers, James, Gaskell, Price
Tries:	Dodd, Smith (2), James, Webster, Blanch (2), Beswick
Goals:	Nanyn (6)

Referee	Peter Taberner	Att: 6,007

NL1 Table

	P	W	D	L	B	F	A	Diff	Pts
Widnes	6	6	0	0	0	290	80	210	18
Whitehaven	6	5	0	1	1	178	96	82	16
Castleford	6	5	0	1	0	295	112	183	15
Leigh	6	3	0	3	2	182	166	16	11
Dewsbury	6	2	0	4	3	131	157	-26	9
Doncaster	6	3	0	3	0	117	238	-121	9
Halifax	6	2	0	4	1	166	189	-23	7
Rochdale	6	2	0	4	0	142	212	-70	6
Batley	6	1	1	4	0	120	257	-137	5
Sheffield	6	0	1	5	1	88	202	-114	3

Loan deal

In a move to aid the development of young forward Adam Sidlow it was announced that he would spend the next month on loan at NL2 side Workington Town. Announcing the decision Steve McCormack added that "this is all part of Adam's long-term development. He is on the fringe of being a first team regular and this spell in Co-operative National League 2 will be good for him. The competition is far more intense than in the Senior Academy and on his return I am expecting him to be looking for a regular spot in the first 17."

CHAPTER FOUR

Half-Time

Shortly after the Castleford match Paul Cook met up with Steve McCormack to gain an insight into the Head Coach's assessment of the season to date. Paul's interview is reproduced here:

When Hull KR ended the Vikings' hopes at the Halliwell Jones Stadium it was a particularly cruel blow for Steve Mc-Cormack. For the third season in succession he had guided a team to the National League Grand Final, only to fall agonisingly at the last hurdle. Two of those defeats came when he was in charge at Whitehaven before taking Widnes to the final at the first attempt. But the achievement of reaching three consecutive finals was little consolation:

"It was a massive disappointment from a personal point of view.

"I was really proud in a way to get through to three finals on the trot and I think a lot of people would probably have swapped places, but to get to the final and get beaten on all those occasions - from a sporting point of view you can't get much lower.

"It was very, very difficult to get over it and it did take a while, luckily I went straight into camp with Scotland last year and we beat Wales so for the first time in three years the season finished on a high, although not from a club point of view."

On each occasion McCormack's side went into the game against clubs who were probably more favoured.

"I think that's true to a certain degree. In the first final against Leigh we were massive underdogs and we were a couple of minutes from winning that, but lost when we went into extra time.

"I think those couple of years for the Whitehaven players, part-time players, to get through to those finals was a massive achievement for them and for the club.

"The club made great strides to do what they did. In the second year they won the League Leader's trophy which was the first trophy in their history and I think the team were satisfied with doing that. I thought for that team, their Grand Final was the week we had paraded the trophy around the ground and the final itself was a big let down.

"I think last year if you look at the team which started the season, then the one which ended it was totally different so I think it was an achievement in itself to get through to the Grand Final."

Widnes had played catch-up with Hull KR throughout the league season, and Rovers had the benefit of a week off before the final while the Vikings had to go through a punishing qualifying game with Whitehaven.

"I felt as though the week leading up to the final we were confident and every one in that side believed we would win, but it was possibly a game too far.

"Hull KR were probably the best side in that division anyway and the Whitehaven game the week before took a lot out of us. With injuries, we hadn't trained a lot with the full team leading up to the final and the way Hull KR started, they were quicker and a bit more youthful than us and fully deserved it. It was heartbreaking."

The intensity of the Whitehaven game was what he had fully expected, and the resulting bumps and bruises disrupted preparation.

"It wasn't a surprise to me as I knew the kind of people we were dealing with at Whitehaven, some fantastic players, but I think in hindsight the week off would have done us a bit of good.

"We had five or six players who couldn't train until the back end of the week and I think it did take a lot out of us. We had quite a few players playing with injections in the final, but that's no excuse for us. We were beaten by a far better side."

In terms of starting again for the coming season, McCormack was aware from past experience that some challenges lay ahead.

"I always knew when I first took over at Whitehaven there were some hard decisions to be made after my first season. We finished sixth and some of the people there had been there a long time and we needed some big changes. I felt as though in the three years we had progressed - finishing sixth, second and first.

"Last year, to a certain degree, I had my hands tied. We had some good players but salary cap wise we were restricted.

"When Steven Vaughan came it helped to bring in players like Jordan James, Oliver Wilkes and Damien Blanch, Gleeson and Moran. They were big changes for us then, and I felt that if we hadn't brought those players in we wouldn't have even made the final.

"We had some very good players from last year so the key, starting in July/August time, was to identify which players we wanted to keep like Beswick, Smith and Blanch, and we looked at players who I'd known from previous seasons and players who had played very well against us, obviously going for youth and pace.

"Scott Grix and Dean Gaskell had always been very good, Lee Doran had torn us apart at our place, and keeping players like Mick Nanyn and Aaron Summers, who I knew from my Whitehaven days, were very good players.

"We just felt as though we needed to freshen the side up and introduce a bit of new blood, more enthusiasm. That's no criticism of people like Terry O'Connor and Barrie McDermott who were fantastic to work with last year.

"I've not mentioned Paul Noone, but I was having a lot of conversations with Paul even when I was on holiday in Spain and he had a lot of options to go to both in SL and National League but he wanted to sign for his home town club, and for me that was good to see because he came for the right reasons.

"The mood at the start was very good. We sat down and had a meeting and I expressed my feeling that the squad we'd built was probably the best I'd ever worked with. The players who were staying were doing so for the right reasons so they knew what the club and the coaching staff were all about, while the players we'd brought in had either played Super League or wanted to play Super League. They all had a burning ambition to reach that level and we felt we had a good blend of youth and experience."

If there had been one criticism of the Vikings' recruitment it was that having let such experienced campaigners as Terry O'Connor and Barrie McDermott, plus fellow prop Ryan Tandy, leave, they were going to be light in the front row. But McCormack says he felt there was sufficient cover within the squad to compensate.

"I spoke with Jordan James early on in the season. I was a little bit disappointed how it had panned out for him in the back row towards the end of the previous year and I felt, along with Andy Haigh, there would be a programme for him to build up into a prop. Oliver Wilkes had played prop for Scotland and Aaron Summers is a player who has never let me down in a big game. He's one of those players who does a lot of work unnoticed.

"The good thing about this game is that everyone has got opinions - players, supporters, on websites and so on - but I always felt we had plenty of cover in the prop situation.

"People like Mike Morrison and Adam Sidlow have stepped up and done a good job. They played in the Challenge Cup against Wigan and performed well and Mick Cassidy as well. I had a good chat with him because he was going to retire, but I persuaded him to stay on another year and I think he's playing his best rugby for us at the moment."

The preparation for the season was also boosted by the Vikings' off-field arrangements being more settled.

"I think a big rap for the backroom staff is deserved as well. We all bought into what we wanted to do, people like Andy Haigh, Tim Holmes, whose own career had finished abruptly and who joined the coaching staff, John Stankevitch and David Banks, plus our new physio all had input in the pre-season.

"We had a settled training ground which was good for us, we were stationed at Total Fitness, and had a good relationship with the council about training on the pitch, and players were coming back fit.

"Last year we were starting with players who had had operations or were injured, but this time we had 17 or 18 who were fit and ready to go which always helps."

With the returning players and new signings on board, the important thing then was to get the right combination, and while the germ of a side may have already been beginning to form, other factors could have played a part.

"You always have an idea about your starting line-up, but pre-season and the Northern Rail games dictate that to a certain degree.

"I always knew what I wanted my structure to be and when I first took over it was difficult to implement that, but as last season progressed we made a few changes and started putting players in position, and from the start of pre-season I had a good idea about what my starting line-up would be."

The start of the campaign saw a good victory at Celtic Crusaders followed closely by a far from satisfactory defeat at Leigh, both in the Northern Rail Cup. One showed the potential in the side, the other became an early piece of motivation and a lesson learned.

"The very first game against Celtic away was a very sticky tie for us. First up, away, in difficult conditions and to go there and win, even though it was a NL2 side, I was really pleased with the way that we played and I think it set the tone.

"I spoke to their coach John Dixon afterwards and he said it was one of the best performances he'd seen from a visiting team for a long time.

"But we played Leigh away and got a good spanking there and all the players and myself got a lot of abuse off our own supporters.

"We were just rubbish. We lost all the collisions. We had a few players missing, Damien Blanch, Mick Nanyn and Dennis Moran but Leigh beat us in every department and rightly or wrongly the fans turned on us. I remember a fan throwing his season ticket at me and I used that as a spur from a coaching point of view.

"We looked in depth at that video and we knew that we couldn't just turn up and expect to win, and I thought that those two games were a big turning point.

"We were under pressure to perform from the very next game and to be fair the players have done that."

That the attitude was spot on was never better exemplified than in the game with Wigan in the Challenge Cup when Widnes gave the Cherry and Whites a real scare, and the first league match of the season with Leigh which saw the Vikings rout a side which had been thought of as a serious contender.

But with a reputation established, McCormack feels teams are determined not to make it easy for Widnes which is why establishing a platform for success is so important.

"The Wigan and Leigh games put a lot of belief into the team. Players in opposition teams now are certainly targeting us as a big side and they aren't going to get broken down in the first five, ten or 15 minutes.

"Even when we have been down at times the players have stuck to their structures and I think that's the sign of a good team and one that's prepared to work.

"This division has got a habit of kicking you in the backside if you start getting carried away with yourself.

"You give your players a framework and patterns of play to fall back on, but they have the freedom to express themselves as long as they don't go too far away from the work we have done in the week."

Despite the battle with Wigan and the heavy defeat of Leigh, McCormack was in no doubt which had been the stand out game in the early weeks of the season.

"The Castleford result was the biggest so far and we went there expecting to win. That's not being arrogant or disrespectful because they are a very good team with a very good coach in Terry Matterson.

"We gave our players individual DVDs of all the Castleford players but the whole emphasis was put on our own performance.

Even though we were under the cosh during the game quite

a bit, to come away with that score was excellent even though we have a lot of improvement in us, as have Cas'."

He also pinpointed a change in the relationship between the team and the fans: "I think Castleford was where the fans really got behind us, and we've seen great support at Sheffield and at Rochdale as well.

"The players have got to be playing well for fans to come out and support them and I think there has been a bit of hangover from what went on at the end of the last season in Super League, and then we didn't get off to the best of starts last season.

"Now I think we're heading in the right direction together again."

He understands that beating Castleford has given Widnes tremendous momentum, but there is always the possibility of a slip.

"It's a long season and we might have a bad spell. That's not being negative it's just what can happen. It's how the players react that's important."

Mick Nanyn prepares to register the 2000th point of his career in the opening League fixture versus Leigh. Mick went on to establish Widnes club records of 434 points and 161 goals in a season during 2007

The Vikings Starlites entertain the fans (above) at a sunny Halton Stadium as Kemik joins the largest crowd of the season against Wigan in the Challenge Cup (below)

The contrasting Don Valley Stadium, Sheffield (above) and the homely Tetleys Stadium, Dewsbury (below) both saw Vikings victories in 2007

Fans and players alike nervously wait for the Northern Rail
Cup Final to get under way at Bloomfield Road, Blackpool

Alan Rae receives his award, for 50 years service to the Supporters Club, from Steve McCormack (above).

Another break by a determined Mark Smith (below)

Poetry in motion - Damien Blanch style (above).

Local boy Paul Noone leads the way home (below)

Bob Beswick prepares to fend off an opponent

Typical power and determination from Ollie Wilkes

CHAPTER FIVE

Second Half

21ˢᵗ May 2007   **Permit granted**

After what seemed like an eternity - in fact it was five weeks – it was finally announced that Danny Lima's work permit had been granted. After several weeks training with no match-day to look forward to, Lima could now stake a claim for inclusion in Steve McCormack's first team.

Coach Steve McCormack was quick to thank local MP Derek Twigg for his assistance in the granting of the permit, and also paid tribute to VIQI who helped to fund the signing. "It's good to know that there are groups of fans who are prepared to work really hard to support the Club. It never ceases to amaze me how much time and effort these people put in and on this occasion I'd like to pass on my thanks, and those from everybody at the Club."

25th May 2007   **Another signing**

In another statement of intent to the fans and the rest of NL1 the Club announced the signing, subject to work permit restrictions, of Joel Penny, the Australian scrum half who had been released by Doncaster Lakers. Although a 'quota' player RFL rules allowed the Australian scrum half to sign for any club, on 'hardship' grounds, as the Lakers had terminated his contract due to their financial situation. The Vikings moved swiftly to take advantage of this situation and add his creative skills to their push for promotion to Super League. The 26 year-old had played for Manly Sea Eagles, South Sydney Rabbitohs and Cronulla Sharks before joining up with Steve McCormack at Whitehaven, and subsequently moving on to Halifax. McCormack added that "he will certainly be a useful addition to the squad and I'm looking forward to working with him again".

27th May 2007 - NRC - Q/F

Rochdale Hornets   0
Widnes Vikings   24

This fixture was transferred to the Halton Stadium as the Hornets' landlords, Rochdale Football Club, were undertaking remedial work on the Spotland pitch.

Following last weeks fantastic win at Castleford, Danny Lima's first inclusion in a Vikings team, and the introduction to the crowd of new signing Joel Penny, an anti-climax was almost inevitable, and so it turned out. There was, however, some interest added to the proceedings as this was the second match to be refereed by a foreign referee of the season - this time from France.

With yet another disappointingly small crowd in the Halton Stadium there was little sign of the confident and expansive rugby that had become the trademark of the 2007 Vikings, and the mood among the fans was as flat as the action on the pitch. However credit must be given to the opposition, and their dogged determination to compete for 80 minutes, although they failed to seriously threaten the Widnes line in the entire game. Steve McCormack succinctly summarised the game: "We set out to get through to the semis and did that. To nil a side is always a bonus…..we played wet weather football and it was like a game of chess at times. Rochdale never deviated from their tactics and gave it their all for 80 minutes."

Frustration was setting in amongst the fans when, after 16 minutes, Damien Blanch raced onto a kick from Dennis Moran, to score out wide, with Mick Nanyn adding a superb conversion from near the touchline. The same three players combined to take the score to 12 – 0 a few minutes before the break. Following a typically forceful Moran tackle, the Hornets winger Balu Fagborun lost control of the ball and Blanch picked it up just inside his own half to sprint unchallenged to the line. Nanyn converted.

After the break play continued in the turgid manner of the first half as the Vikings had to wait until midway through the second period to add to their score. The ball had again been dropped by Fagborun when it was collected by former Hornet Lee Doran, who set off deep into Hornets territory before Moran again played his part by getting the ball to the supporting Andy Kirk, who joyfully stretched for the line. This was Kirk's second try in three matches, and he was proving a more than capable deputy for the suspended Toa Kohe-Love in both defence and attack. The final score of the day came fifteen minutes from the end as Ian Webster ran through a tiring and beaten Hornets defence.

Some five weeks after his signing the Widnes faithful finally got their chance to run the rule over Danny Lima. Whilst the start to his Widnes career was subdued the fans were expecting more from the big forward once he attained match fitness. The game itself was certainly not a classic, but in retrospect it allowed the Vikings to display their tactical awareness in playing to the conditions and grinding out a result on the back of an excellent defensive performance.

Vikings:	Grix: Blanch, Kirk, Nanyn, Dodd, Moran, Webster, Cassidy, Smith, Wilkes, Doran, Noone, Beswick. Subs: Summers, James, Gaskell, Lima
Tries:	Blanch (2), Kirk, Webster
Goals:	Nanyn (4)
Hornets:	Hulse; Andrews, Patterson, King, Fagborun; Svabic, Hasty; Bailey, McConnell, Smith, Gorski, Baldwin, Goulden. Subs: Giles, Marsh, Corcoran, Benjafield
Referee:	Thierry Alibert (Fra) Att: 2,382

31ˢᵗ May 2007   **Three scrum halves !**

Today's news releases from the Halton Stadium related to not one but three scrum halves!

In stark contrast to the Danny Lima saga the club was in the happy position of announcing that Joel Penny's work permit had been granted - in just seven days – to allow him to be available for selection for the next match.

It was also announced that two further players had gone

out on loan – Andy Kain and Martin Keavney. Kain, having dropped to third choice scrum half behind new recruit Penny and Ian Webster, would spend the remainder of the season with NL2 side Featherstone Rovers, whilst Keavney joined his Academy colleague Adam Sidlow at Workington Town to gain valuable competitive experience.

1st June 2007   **Rugby League World**

An indication of the standards being set, consistently, by Widnes Vikings was reflected in a feature on the top 50 players outside Super League in the June edition of the magazine. There were ten members of the current Vikings squad included in this elite group, which was headed by Castleford's Danny Brough. The players, with their rankings, were Mark Smith (2), Dennis Moran (3), Bob Beswick (5), Oliver Wilkes (11), Mick Nanyn (15), Scott Grix (16), Toa Kohe-Love (20), Damien Blanch (26), Paul Noone (28) and Mick Cassidy (31).

3rd June 2007 - NL1

Widnes Vikings	**56**
Sheffield Eagles	**10**

The combination of a continued winning run, good weather, and the debut of Joel Penny failed to entice the missing thousands back to the Halton Stadium. It beggared belief that such a strong 'rugby town' could still not produce attendances that the brand of fast, skilful rugby the players were consistently producing, so richly deserved!

What eventually became yet another convincing victory for the Vikings, began as many other matches had done – with the opposition chalking up an early advantage. In previous seasons such an early reverse would have led to a chorus of boos and hyper-criticism but the regular Vikings supporters of 2007 had found a new resilience and confidence to match that of the team.

The absence of Scott Grix and Paul Noone through injury seemed to unsettle the balance of the side, but gradually they assumed control, and began to breach the Eagles defence at will. Although the referee wiped off an Ollie Wilkes try – to award Widnes a penalty – the Vikings continued to surge forward at every opportunity and after 20 minutes Wilkes got his reward when feeding off a strong run from Mick Nanyn to open the host's account. Nanyn ensured full value with the first of his eight goals of the afternoon. Having got their noses in front the Vikings soon extended their lead when, with his first touch of the ball in a Widnes shirt, Joel Penny slipped a short pass to Jordan James to crash over under the posts in the 30th minute. The half closed with Nanyn, looking far more assured with the ball in hand than last season, breaking the defensive line and converting his own try.

After repelling a strong opening to the second half from the Eagles the Vikings extended their lead, with two tries in as many minutes. Wilkes took advantage of a slick passing movement at speed between Penny, Nanyn and Bob Beswick, before an improving Gareth Price off-loaded to Dennis Moran for the stand-off to race in in typical fashion from just inside the opposition half. Wilkes was again put in by Beswick to complete the first hat-trick of his career on 55 minutes. Putting in arguably his best performance in a Widnes shirt, Aaron Summers made a strong run deep into opposition territory only to be thwarted just short of the line, but in the 60th minute he conjured a clever off-load to put Gavin Dodd in from close range, with Nanyn's conversion taking the lead to 40 - 10.

On a day of crisp passing and slick off-loads pride of place should go to Dean Gaskell. As the Sheffield defence shunted him towards the touchline the diminutive winger somehow conjured an amazing off-load to the supporting Andy Kirk, who rode two tackles before passing inside for Nanyn to stroll through for his second try. Neat footwork in a crowded defence then allowed Penny to score under the posts from five metres out before the barn-storming Nanyn forced his way over in the corner, to complete his hat-trick and return a personal tally of 28 points.

After another entertaining game Steve McCormack commented: "I was delighted for Oliver Wilkes and also thought Mick Nanyn had one of his best ever games. Some of the tries in the second half were of the highest quality and show that from 1-17 we have a highly skilled outfit."

Vikings:	Dodd: Blanch, Kirk, Nanyn, Gaskell, Moran, Webster, Cassidy, Smith, Wilkes, Doran, Summers, Beswick. Subs: Penny, Lima, James, Price
Tries:	Wilkes (3), James, Nanyn (3), Moran, Dodd, Penny
Goals:	Nanyn (8)
Eagles:	Woodcock; Mills, Ford, Reid, Hurst, Lindsay, Brown, Stringer, Cook, Corcoran, Brown, Trayler, Hayes. Subs: Brambani, Hepworth, Holdstock, Buckenham
Tries:	Ford (2)
Goal:	Woodcock
Referee:	Jamie Leahy Att: 2,837

10th June 2007 - NL1

Doncaster	4
Widnes Vikings	90

When the fixtures were announced such a one-sided affair could not have been envisaged for the first visit to the
new Keepmoat Stadium. As it turned out the 1200 fans who
turned up witnessed the biggest winning margin in Widnes'
history, as the home fans feared liquidation within days. The
performance of Joel Penny - released because of those financial
problems - only served to rub salt in the wounds of the die-
hard Doncaster fans.

With less than a minute on the clock Gavin Dodd's record-
breaking afternoon (38 points in the match) was under way
when Scott Grix put him through for a 50 metre run to the
line to register the opening try. Assuming the kicking duties
of the absent Mick Nanyn, Dodd then added the first of his
thirteen goals before going on to complete a hat-trick of tries
which took him to 100 points for the season, and through the
400 career points barrier.

Damien Blanch, taking Nanyn's place in the centres, was
next to cross the whitewash when Aaron Summers' pass put
him clear to score, before Summers and Penny did the spade
work for Dennis Moran and Bob Beswick to create the space
for Dodd to get his second try after only fifteen minutes. Three
minutes later the Vikings were 'ahead of the clock' when Beswick released Ollie Wilkes to charge through the defence and
round the fullback to score. Dodd's conversion took the score
to 22 - 0. Further tries from Penny and Andy Kirk, either side
of Adebisi's consolation effort for Doncaster, allowed the Vikings to ease into a 34 - 4 lead at the interval. Penny had done
much to engineer his own score when, following a break by

Mark Smith, he twisted out of a tackle to touch down, while Kirk's effort came after Dean Gaskell had passed inside to put him through.

Throughout the afternoon the creative quartet of Smith, Moran, Penny and Beswick had tormented the home side with tremendous support from their team-mates. The second-half became even more of a procession with the visitors scoring at a rate of nearly one-and-a half points per minute. First Dodd completed his hat-trick on 44 minutes, when Ian Webster intercepted a Lakers pass to set up Blanch who off-loaded for the winger to score. Straight from the re-start the Lakers conceded a penalty from which Smith created the opportunity for Summers to score a rare try. Having smelt the whitewash Summers came back for more when he was in the right place to benefit from another Smith-inspired move which allowed Beswick to put the second-rower in to complete an unlikely brace. Dodd's conversion brought the score to 52 - 4 as the winger unwittingly edged towards his record points haul.

Smith was again involved in the next score, on fifty minutes, as straight from the kick-off he supported a forceful run from Mick Cassidy before playing in Penny for his second try of the afternoon. Another strong break, this time from Cassidy's front row partner Wilkes, put Blanch in for his second try, and extend the lead to 58 points. In the 56th minute Kirk, playing well in the continued absence of Kohe-Love, was baulked in his attempt to reach the line, but Gaskell darted over from dummy-half. Before Blanch and Penny completed their hat-tricks Grix made up for missing an earlier golden opportunity when he collected a pass from Penny, at the base of the scrum, to leave the home defence trailing in his wake as he ran in from 80 metres out. The hat-trick tries duly came from Blanch, courtesy of a pass from Beswick, and Penny who linked with Grix before touching down, while the final try of the afternoon came when Webster created the opportunity for Wilkes to score.

Whilst naturally pleased with the performance Steve Mc-Cormack prophetically added in his after-match comments that "there is still room for improvement and we need to focus on these areas before we travel to Halifax on Thursday." The coach was also "delighted for Gavin Dodd and to break a record held jointly by Jonathan Davies and Andy Currier is a superb achievement."

Lakers:	Skelton, Close, Buttery, Leaf, Adebisi, McLocklan, Speak, Garmston, Bettinson, Benson, Lawton, Hesketh, Green. Subs: Carey, Mills, Castle, Rowe
Try:	Adebisi
Vikings:	Grix, Gaskell, Kirk, Blanch, Dodd, Moran, Penny, Cassidy, Smith, Wilkes, Doran, Summers, Beswick. Subs: Webster, Lima, James, Price
Tries:	Dodd (3), Blanch (3), Wilkes (2), Penny (3), Kirk, Summers (2), Gaskell, Grix
Goals:	Dodd (13)
Referee:	Steve Ganson Att: 1,248

Second Half

Halifax	12
Widnes Vikings	6

Featured again as the live game on Sky Television Widnes came crashing to - a very soggy - earth following their exploits against a weak Doncaster side four days earlier. In the process they lost their 100% record in the League to put to the sword the unrealistic expectations that had built up in some quarters about remaining unbeaten throughout the league campaign. In a hard fought match it was the home side who adapted to the conditions better and consistently turned the Vikings defence as a result of their excellent kicking game. Proof that it was not all one-way traffic was the post-match praise heaped upon the Halifax defence - Widnes had the possession but could not make the vital breakthrough until the 73rd minute.

It could have been so different however if the visitors had capitalised on two good opportunities before the home side opened the scoring on 21 minutes. Joel Penny, playing against a former club for the second time in four days, tried to put Bob Beswick through in the Vikings'first attack, but the vice-captain just failed to grasp the wet ball with the line beckoning only feet away from him. Then, on 20 minutes, the video referee denied Scott Grix the opening score when Lee Doran was adjudged to have been off-side when a kick from Dennis Moran struck him on its way to Grix.

Halifax immediately responded to this let off when in their next attack a grubber from Penkywicz ironically ricocheted off a Widnes boot, playing Ball on-side, for the Halifax man to score. The hosts continued to build pressure on the Vikings defence and were perhaps unfortunate not to increase their lead before half-time when Grix failed to gather a bomb, injuring his arm in the process and was not able to continue. After the break Halifax came roaring out of the traps to put Widnes under constant pressure which led to them adding a second try in the 45th minute.

The Vikings fought back to gain some possession and form but failed to capitalise on the half-chances that came their way. In addition they had a second try disallowed by the video referee who adjudged that Ian Webster had not grounded the ball correctly. Minutes later the deficit was increased to 12- 0 thanks to a penalty conceded some 25 metres out. The Vikings finally managed to trouble the scorers when, following a period of sustained pressure, Mark Smith kicked through for Webster to draw another decision from the video referee - this time in Widnes' favour. Although finishing the game in the ascendancy the Vikings' were unable to force the draw, but gathered the consolation of their first bonus point.

"I've no complaints about the result" said Steve McCormack, adding "all credit to Halifax who played the conditions better than we did. Graham Holroyd and Ian Watson's kicking games were outstanding, they kicked us to death. In fact Halifax outplayed us in all departments. I thought we defended really well but when we had possession we failed to control the ball and our completion rate was not good enough. What we need to do now is react positively and a Northern Rail Cup Semi-Final against Castleford is an ideal opportunity to do so."

Halifax:	Gibson, George, Roberts, Varkulis, Greenwood, Holroyd, Watson, Southern, Penkywicz, Watene, Heaton, Smith, Joseph. Subs: Hoare, Larder, Ball, Shickell
Tries:	Ball, Larder
Goals:	Holroyd (2)

Vikings:	Grix, Blanch, Kohe-Love, Nanyn, Dodd, Moran, Penny, Cassidy, Smith, Wilkes, Doran, Noone, Beswick. Subs: Summers, James, Kirk, Webster
Try:	Webster
Goal:	Nanyn
Referee:	Jamie Leahy Att: 2,142

NL1 Table

	P	W	D	L	B	F	A	Diff	Pts
Widnes	9	8	0	1	1	442	106	336	25
Castleford	9	8	0	1	0	408	149	259	24
Whitehaven	9	7	0	2	1	282	152	130	22
Leigh	9	5	0	4	3	260	209	51	18
Halifax	9	4	0	5	1	250	233	17	13
Dewsbury	9	3	0	6	4	188	263	-75	13
Rochdale	9	3	0	6	0	184	282	-98	9
Batley	9	2	1	6	0	190	367	-177	8
Sheffield	9	1	1	7	2	137	285	-148	7
Doncaster *	9	3	0	6	0	141	436	-295	3

* 6 points deducted for entering Administration

18th June 2007   **Twin targets**

Preparing for the Northern Rail Cup semi-final against Castleford Tigers Steve McCormack identified a Cup Final appearance as a building block towards a Super League return. The Vikings' coach took the opportunity to reaffirm that his aim was to reach the Final of any competition that the club entered, and with a place in the Final at Blackpool's Bloomfield Road at stake he added "We aim to win every competition we enter and the Northern Rail Cup is no different. It's going to be a massive match against Castleford and we're really looking forward to it."

The clash at the Halton Stadium was to bring together the top two teams in NL1 with Widnes arguably holding the upper hand after convincingly winning the recent league fixture at The Jungle, although McCormack was quick to point out that that result would have no bearing on the outcome of the semi-final. "It is bound to produce a competitive tie....Widnes has yet to play in the Northern Rail Cup Final and that's something we aim to put right.... we want our fans to experience that special day out at Bloomfield Road" he added.

Coach moves on

The club also announced that Senior Academy Coach John Stankevitch had resigned from his position with the club. Vikings' Head Coach Steve McCormack thanked Stankevitch "for all the work he had done over the last 18 months as both Senior Academy coach and as an assistant at first team games. He worked tirelessly over this period and on behalf of everybody at the Club I'd like to wish him every success in his future career."

The following day Stankevitch was duly appointed as Head Coach by the new owners of Doncaster, confirming the rumours that had appeared in the media. Looking forward to bringing his new team to the Halton Stadium some six weeks later Stankevitch sent the following message to Widnes and its supporters:

"I'd like to thank all the players, coaching staff and office staff for all the help they've given me over the last two years. Widnes was my first ever coaching role and I can't thank the club enough for giving me that opportunity.

"However, there is a limited number of Head Coach posts in the professional game and when the opportunity comes along you have to look seriously at it. It's an enormous challenge and one I'm really looking forward to. We're currently bottom of National League 1 and favourites for relegation so the only way is up. I will be commuting to Doncaster so will try to get down to Widnes' games when I can."

24th June 2007   - NRC - S/F

Widnes Vikings	**18**
Castleford Tigers	**12**

"We're all going to Black-pool, na-na na na, We're all going to Black-pool ………"

With accompaniment from 'the drummer' the fans sang their way out of the Halton Stadium as the Vikings qualified for their first Cup Final since a Wembley crowd in excess of 77,000 saw them go down 20 - 14 to Wigan in the Challenge Cup Final of 1993.

Thanks to an impressive 'away' following - boosted by many sporting a variety of Yorkshire based Super League replica shirts - a much healthier attendance was recorded at the Halton Stadium for arguably the most important single match since the disappointment of last year's Grand Final defeat. However this was not to be a repeat of the flowing rugby fest that saw the Vikings home at The Jungle in the recent league encounter, but rather a hard-fought victory based on excellent defence.

The match started in a promising vein as, taking possession from the kick-off, the Vikings went onto the attack and had much the better of the opening exchanges, forcing two 'drop-outs' in the first few minutes to keep the visitors under pressure. The tense atmosphere suddenly relaxed - for the home fans - as in the ninth minute Penny fed Moran around the Tigers' 10 metre line. The Stand-off's reputation with ball in hand immediately drew three defenders to him as Ollie Wilkes raced through in close support. Moran's crisp pass to the in-form Prop enabled him to score his sixth try in his last four games, with Mick Nanyn notching the first of his five goals to maximise the lead. Ten minutes later, after repelling some determined play from the Tigers, Bob Beswick, finding himself out wide on the left, some fifteen metres from the Tigers' line, slipped a reverse pass to Nanyn who cut inside and barged his way past several defenders to score. Nanyn converted his own try, and then added a penalty to take the lead to 14 - 0 with just 23 minutes on the clock.

Disrupted by three players leaving the field to have attention to head wounds, Widnes failed to capitalise on chances to hammer home their superiority, allowing the opposition to mount a fight-back which resulted in two tries in six minutes, and swung the pendulum in the Tigers' favour as half-time approached. After some sloppy play in midfield Castleford gained possession 20 metres from the Widnes line to launch a concerted attack. Defending resolutely on their line Widnes forced a loose pass but the Tigers' Boyle reacted quickest to force the ball over from close in. Worse was to come as Brough was put through, by a forward pass, for Boyle to again reap the benefit despite the attention of Moran. Having been on top for most of the first period it was the Vikings who were hanging on for the whistle, and went to the dressing room with their advantage reduced to 14 - 12.

Despite the best creative efforts of Joel Penny, Mark Smith, Moran, and McGoldrick and Brough for the visitors, the second half became a 'master class' in the art of defence. Although the Vikings had the territorial advantage they were unable to add to their score, with the exception of two Nanyn penalties, which extended their lead to a nervous six points. In an attempt to find the extra breathing space as full-time approached, Moran, Smith and Penny all failed with attempts for a one-pointer.

As Widnes hung on and Castleford strived for an equalising score the pressure of the occasion was plainly getting to both sets of players - and the fans in the stands - as the final minutes were played out in an almost deathly quiet as the collective breath was held until the final hooter sounded. But even then there was still time for a final scare. As the Vikings players all seemed to stop, expecting the final whistle, Paul Noone - many people's selection as Man of the Match - flapped at a loose ball instead of dropping on it to end the game. A Tigers player then kicked the ball sixty metres towards the Widnes line and sprinted after it, only to be beaten by the alert Penny who ran the ball 'dead' to cement a place in the Final, and finally signal the chorus of *"We're all going to Black-pool............"*.

Placing the credit for the victory on his side's defensive effort Steve McCormack added "that's as good as you can get in this division. It was as physical as anything I have seen all year, in any league."

Vikings: Grix; Blanch, Kohe-Love, Nanyn, Dodd, Moran, Penny, Cassidy, Smith, Wilkes, Summers, Noone, Beswick. Subs: Webster, Doran, James, Lima.

Tries:	Wilkes, Nanyn
Goals:	Nanyn (5)

Tigers:	Saxton; Donlan, Shenton, Dixon, Wainwright, McGoldrick, Brough, Leafa, Henderson, Huby, Guttenbeil, Charles, Clayton. Subs: Westerman, Glassie, Boyle, Higgins.
Tries:	Boyle (2)
Goals:	Brough (2)

Referee:	Gareth Hewer	Att: 5,338

26th June 2007   **'Mid-Term Report'**

Following positive comments from the players after the 'Squad Night' held in pre-season the Supporters Club hosted a 'Mid-Term Report', where coach, players and fans could again meet in a social setting. With immaculate timing - just two days after beating Castleford to qualify for the Northern Rail Cup Final - Steve McCormack and the players received a rapturous welcome from everyone present. Mark Naughton and Gary McGrath again MC'd the event which was also attended by Adam Sidlow and Martin Keavney, both of whom had recently moved on loan to Workington for the remainder of the season. Recent signings Danny Lima and Joel Penny also made their 'social' debuts for the club and it was readily apparent that they had already integrated into the happy atmosphere of the dressing room. This was particularly highlighted by players mockingly falling asleep when Lima took to the microphone!

During the evening an award was made to Gavin Dodd by

the Supporters Club to mark his points scoring record in the recent victory at Doncaster. His haul of 3 tries and 13 goals gave him a total of 38 points for the match, establishing a new club record for points scored in a single match. Apparently unaware that he was about to set a new record until a message came on with the kicking tee, 'Doddy' admitted that he thought that Mick Nanyn was the current record holder. He had in fact surpassed the previous record of 34 points jointly held by Jonathon Davies and Andy Currier.

In the days leading up to the event fans had been given the opportunity to register questions to be put to the coach and his players. As a selection of these were read out by our hosts McCormack was able to give an insight into some of his match-day routines, and in particular how he used a 'laptop' to re-run key incidents on DVD as part of his half-time talks.

The coach also felt that there were still improvements to come from the team despite their position at the top of the league, adding that they are "a good bunch of players to work with" with an excellent team spirit.

After the coach and the players had taken their turn with the microphone answering questions from the fans, Mark Naughton introduced a special award to be made to a Vikings stalwart. A surprised Alan Rae stepped forward to a stirring round of applause to receive a gift-set of a Decanter and Glasses (with the obligatory bottle of Whisky) to mark fifty years service with the Supporters Club. Receiving his award from Steve McCormack a "shocked and speechless" Alan commented that it was an honour to receive an award for something that he had enjoyed doing for all those years.

Following a week of speculation it was formally announced that Tim Holmes would be taking over as Senior Academy Coach from the recently departed John Stankevitch. Intending to carry on with the good work of his predecessor the popular

Holmes was "made up" to receive the offer and reflected that "the injury happened .... and it's time to move on".

1st July 2007 - NL1

Widnes Vikings	32
Rochdale Hornets	0

Finally the attendance approached a figure that the players deserved - thanks to an excellent initiative between the Club and Sponsors Hattons Solicitors. Some three weeks before the match it was announced that all Season Tickets holders would be able to claim three complimentary tickets for this match to pass on to lapsed, or new supporters, in an attempt to boost attendances at the Halton Stadium. In excess of 2,500 tickets were issued, and although some naturally ended up in the hands of 'regulars' it would appear that the exercise was a success as the average home attendance, in all competitions, prior to this match was 3,277 (3,106 for NL1). The combination of 1,600 extra fans, and the temporary re-location of some 'North Standers' to the East Stand at a special price of £5, certainly made the match-day atmosphere a bit more real.

For the third time this season the Vikings were made to work hard for victory over a Hornets side that included former Widnes players Chris Giles and Gary Hulse. A solid defensive effort ensured the points came to the Halton Stadium but also enabled the Vikings to achieve a second successive clean sheet against their opponents. Whilst the visitors were again 'shut out', rarely looking like scoring, they were nonetheless a difficult team to break down for a Widnes side again not firing on all cylinders in wet conditions.

They did however get off to a good start with both wingers

scoring in the opening fifteen minutes. In the fourth minute Gavin Dodd capitalised on a succession of fast, crisp passing when Mick Nanyn played him in to score in the corner, before Dean Gaskell dived into the corner on the right wing some ten minutes later having been put through by Dennis Moran. Nanyn added the 'extras' with an excellent kick from the touchline. The next try came on seventeen minutes when the rampaging Ollie Wilkes benefited from an off-load from skipper Mark Smith and powered his way over the line before the final try of the half came from Scott Grix as the fullback collected a deft ball from Nanyn, and his nimble footwork took him past the Rochdale defence. With Nanyn only achieving a rare 50% success rate with his kicks the Vikings went in at half-time with a 20 - 0 advantage.

After a dour ten minutes the second half came to life when the Vikings again scored two tries within the space of three minutes, the first being claimed by Joel Penny who took advantage of a gap created by the Hornets' on-rushing defence to score by the posts in the 52nd minute. Three minutes later the Vikings gained ground thanks to a strong 20 metre run from the much improved Gareth Price, and from the play-the-ball Smith fed Ian Webster who cashed in to score his tenth try of the season. Nanyn converted both tries to take the score to 32 - 0.

Steve McCormack commented after the game that the increased attendance had given the players a lift, and hopefully they would all return for the next home match. Many of the stay-away fans had cited the runaway victories as the reason for not attending matches. On that logic (?) this hard-fought encounter should tempt them back - or would it be case of 'see - they're not as good as they think they are'! Perhaps these fair-weather fans would return to the fold after enjoying their day in the limelight at Blackpool !

Vikings:	Grix, Gaskell, Kohe-Love, Nanyn, Dodd, Moran, Penny, James, Smith, Price, Doran, Wilkes, Beswick. Subs: Webster, Cassidy, Kirk, Lima
Tries:	Dodd, Gaskell, Wilkes, Grix, Penny, Webster
Goals:	Nanyn (4)
Hornets:	Giles, Andrews, Marsh, King, Fagborun, Hasty, Hulse, Bailey, McConnell, Smith, Gorski, Baldwin, Goulden. Subs: Gledhill, Benjifield, Blanchard, Norman
Referee:	Craig Halloran Att: 4,879

5th July 2007 - NL1

Dewsbury Rams	**10**
Widnes Vikings	**50**

In a game played in atrocious conditions throughout the Vikings again had the benefit of a marvellous turnout of travelling support that had journeyed along the M62 to outnumber their hosts in the compact, yet strangely rustic setting of the Tetley's Stadium.

Widnes' sixth appearance before the television cameras of 2007 showcased an outstanding display of teamwork in their final build up to the Northern Rail Cup Final. A match in which the Vikings adapted to the conditions better than their hosts saw Dean Gaskell take the individual post-match accolades. His inspiring performance, deputising for the injured Damien

Blanch, which included a hat-trick of tries certainly gave Steve McCormack a selection headache prior to the following week's Cup Final. Having conceded the almost customary first try - to an exciting Rams move as on the fifth tackle they moved the ball with speed and precision virtually the length of the pitch to score in the corner - the Vikings struck back with their own passing game on the back of some excellent forward play.

They drew level when the Rams' Preece failed to deal with a Dennis Moran bomb. From the resultant scrum Moran passed wide to the supporting Toa Kohe-Love who put Gaskell through to score by the flag. Just three minutes later Preece muffed another bomb under pressure from Jordan James, who gained possession. From the play-the-ball Joel Penny sidestepped four defenders to score under the posts - Mick Nanyn adding the extras. Widnes then scored another quick-fire brace of tries to establish a commanding lead shortly after the half-hour mark. Moving deep into Rams territory on the back of a penalty the ball was fed out to the left. When it came back in-field Jordan James was the first to react to Bob Beswick's grubber to score by the posts. Then on 33 minutes the Rams attempted to play the ball across-field, from a scrum inside their 10 metre line, only for the greasy ball to be dropped 'in-goal'. Scott Grix merely had to take two strides to ground the loose ball.

Coming out for the second half with a lead of 20 - 4 the Vikings wasted no time in further extending their lead when Gaskell again scored in the corner. Ollie Wilkes had made a strong run into the opposition half for Smith to link with Moran whose long pass cut out two players on its way to Gaskell. On an evening of inconsistent kicking Nanyn converted his most difficult chance of the match from the touchline. The next score was a trademark effort, in the 50th minute, from Moran as he intercepted a Rams pass on his own 10 metre line and sprinted unchallenged to touch down under the sticks - finding time to smile to the fans on the way! Nanyn's kick sailed over the bar and into the adjacent field.

Following a strong run in his own half Nanyn was then on hand to take an excellent pass from Beswick, deep in opposition territory, to score the Vikings' seventh try of the game in the 50th minute. This score owed much to the good handling skills of Gaskell and Mick Cassidy that had kept the ball alive in mid-field. Former Widnes player Dean Lawford then took advantage of slack defensive play on the hour to score, but this was no more than an irritation as the Vikings raised their game again to run in a further three tries in the last ten minutes.

The first came in the 71st minute after Moran had dislodged the ball in a typically forceful tackle five metres from the Rams' line. The ball was then passed along the line and then back to the centre where Moran made ground before slipping a short pass to Kohe-Love for the Kiwi centre to score his twelfth try of the season. Gaining possession from the kick-off the Vikings then moved straight down the pitch for Ian Webster to score whilst sitting on the ground! Strong running from Gareth Price and Aaron Summers created the field position for Webster to take a short pass from Beswick, turn two defenders while being dragged to the ground, and extended his arm to score. With just two minutes left a seemingly surprised Beswick took an off-load from Summers 40 metres out to set up a fine passing movement involving Smith, Grix and Kohe-Love to put Gaskell in for his hat-trick.

| **Rams:** | Preece, Powell, Maloney(F), Maun, Buchanan, Walker, Lawford, Hobson, Finn, Maloney(D), Crouthers, Robinson, Bretherton, Subs: Haigh, Kelly, Hulme, Southwell |

Tries:	Maloney(F), Lawford
Goals:	Finn

Vikings:	Grix, Gaskell, Kohe-Love, Nanyn, Dodd, Moran, Penny, Cassidy, Smith, Wilkes, Doran, Noone, Beswick. Subs: Summers, James, Webster, Price
Tries:	Gaskell (3), Penny, James, Grix, Moran, Nanyn, Kohe-Love, Webster
Goals:	Nanyn (5)

Referee:	Gareth Hewer	Att: 1,885

Loan deal

It was announced that Darryl Cardiss had signed for Batley Bulldogs on an initial one month loan deal. Unfortunately, for all concerned, this proved to be a short-lived arrangement when, in only his second match Cardiss picked up a shoulder injury that brought a premature end to his season.

11th July 2007   **Lima leaves**

In the lead up to Sunday's Cup Final a surprising announcement from the Club confirmed that Danny Lima had left the club. During Lima's brief stay with the Vikings he had failed to have the impact on the team that had been hoped for, and he was understood to have decided to follow interests outside the game. It was ironic that, having waited five weeks for his work permit to be granted, his 'game time' was restricted to very short bursts over a period of just six weeks.

15th July 2007 - NRC - Final
Bloomfield Road, Blackpool

Whitehaven	6
Widnes Vikings	54

From an unlikely beginning in the February snow of Bridgend this 'rail' journey terminated on a day of summer rain in Blackpool. Undaunted, we were all glad to be there, and for some Widnesians the party had started in this famous old town on Saturday night! However it really started to buzz when a mixture of trains, coaches and cars disgorged their passengers into a leaden-skied Blackpool on Sunday morning, the resort becoming a sea of black and white as Vikings fans really got into the party mood. The natural aromas of Blackpool were momentarily extinguished from the senses as the atmosphere seemed full of an expectancy that, falling just short of over-confidence, was almost tangible as the black and white hordes made their way to the stadium. Even the stewards who diligently confiscated the 'poles' from our flags could not spoil the mood, on the day that Steve McCormack finally collected a winners' medal!

The stay-away fans had long ignored the brand of confident, expansive rugby that had been on display, home and away, all season, but having turned up for the 'big match' they were treated to a scintillating performance that even surpassed the expectations of the faithful, as the opposition were simply blown away. From 1 to 17 there were excellent performances from the Vikings whose kit matched this 'red-letter day'.

With the Widnes fans dominating the off-pitch contest their heroes were very much on the front foot as from the kick-off they confidently carried the fight to Whitehaven, who barely got out of their own half in the first period. Even the most die-hard Vikings fan could not have expected the match to be so one-sided as the destination of the Cup was effectively wrapped up after a blistering first half in which it was difficult to recall any errors from a totally dominant Widnes outfit. It was plain to see from the kick-off that the game plan of Whitehaven was to spoil and slow the game down at every opportunity - a game plan that ultimately failed miserably.

The show, for that's what it became, got under way in the 6th minute when one of many penalties conceded by Whitehaven, for a high tackle on Scott Grix, enabled Widnes to start the next 'set' only 25 metres from the opposition line. Quick passing from Mark Smith and Dennis Moran gave Grix the opportunity to cut out two defenders with a pass to

Toa Kohe-Love to score a try which Mick Nanyn converted from the touchline. Another penalty gave Nanyn the chance to stretch the lead to eight points with a straightforward kick from 22 metres in the 13th minute. Only three minutes later, from a play-the-ball on their own 20 metre line, Grix and Moran played in the supporting Kohe-Love who ran deep into 'Haven territory with Grix and Damien Blanch roaring up in support. With the defence seeming to anticipate the pass to the speedy Blanch Kohe-Love passed inside to enable Grix to sprint in for his eighteenth try of the season.

The Cumbrians were already fading fast under the constant pressure from the Vikings and when they put a kick out 'on the full' in the 20th minute Aaron Summers and Jordan James gained a strong territorial advantage. Smith and Moran again combined for the latter to isolate the defence with a long pass to Blanch on the wing who duly scored. Nanyn extended the lead to 18 - 0 with another excellent kick from the touchline. With the match punctuated with scores every few minutes the public address announcer was again called into action when Nanyn converted yet another penalty, this time for a grapple tackle on Smith, on 24 minutes.

The sequence continued in the 28th minute as Joel Penny, who had only passed a fitness test just before the match, jinked his way towards the line only to be halted just short. From the re-start Bob Beswick fired a long pass to the advancing Nanyn, for the big centre to sidestep his marker, and score with ease against his former employers, with his conversion taking the score to a commanding 26 - 0. The final score of the half came when Penny took an off-load from James near the half-way line and set off on a run down centre-field, only to be hauled down again just two metres out. From the play-the-ball it was again Moran who cut out several defenders with a pass to Lee Doran who stepped inside one challenge before strolling across the line.

Nanyn unusually missed with his kick. As the hooter sounded Smith gathered his ebullient team together for their customary 'huddle' while a demoralised Whitehaven trudged off to the dressing room on the wrong end of a 30 - 0 scoreline.

Joel Penny was withdrawn at half-time to protect his injured ankle, being replaced by Ian Webster. However the rout continued just two minutes into the second half when Moran, on his own 40 metre line, collected a rebound from his own kick to sprint through the 'Haven defence before giving his captain the opportunity to race through to score by the posts. In the 46th minute the Vikings scored again as, from a scrum some 15 metres out, Moran passed to Kohe-Love, who drew three defenders before making an instinctive pass outside where Blanch steamed through to again score in the corner. On the hour the fans' dream of a 'whitewash' was shattered as Whitehaven finally broke through from close range for Rudd to score in front of those 'Haven fans who were still in the stadium. Many had by this time begun the journey home.

This was, however, only a temporary interruption to the Widnes steamroller as, courtesy of Nanyn converting yet another penalty, the score moved on to 42 - 6 with fifteen minutes remaining.

Even though the contest had long been over the Vikings pushed home their dominance with further tries in the 71st and 75th minutes. First, Paul Noone, receiving an off-load from James on half-way, showed an impressive change of pace, and direction, to dart through the defence before laying off to Ian Webster, who immediately set Moran free to score under the posts from 25 metres out. The final try of the day came on the back of yet another barnstorming run from Ollie Wilkes. Smith played in Nanyn who off-loaded near the line for the supporting Dean Gaskell, selected ahead of the unlucky Gavin Dodd, to score. In converting both efforts Nanyn took his tally to 22 points - a record for the Northern Rail Cup Final - and also reach the 700 point mark in his Widnes career.

As the after-match proceedings began Dennis Moran was first up the stairs to collect his Man of the Match award from Heidi Mottram, Managing Director of Northern Rail. He then returned alongside Steve McCormack and his team-mates to collect their winner's medals before the travelling army of Widnes fans roared their approval as Mark Smith lifted the Northern Rail Cup. Still with one eye on a Grand Final appearance in October, McCormack and his players savoured the victory as they posed for photographs and paraded the trophy around the ground, but it was probably an even sweeter moment for Toa Kohe-Love. The Kiwi had not picked up a winner's medal in his long and illustrious career but made up for it today with a try and two 'assists' in what was his 250th career appearance.

Whitehaven:	Broadbent, Calvert, Elbeck, Jackson (R), Maden, Joe, Duffy, Trindall, Smith (A), Fatialofa, Miller, Fletcher, Rudd. Subs: Sice, Mattinson, Jackson (M), Teare
Try:	Rudd
Goal:	Rudd
Vikings:	Grix, Blanch, Kohe-Love, Nanyn, Gaskell, Moran, Penny, Cassidy, Smith, Wilkes, Doran, Noone, Beswick. Subs: Summers, James, Webster, Price
Tries:	Kohe-Love, Grix, Blanch (2), Nanyn, Doran, Smith, Moran, Gaskell
Goals:	Nanyn (9)
Referee:	Jamie Leahy Att: 8,236

The Vikings' first trophy since 2001 had also produced the first winners' medal, following several near misses, for the amiable Steve McCormack. The Head Coach explained to Paul Cook that he was in no doubt that winning the Northern Rail Cup fitted in to the season's overall plan:

The Northern Rail Cup proved, without a doubt, that Widnes were the form team of the National League at that stage of the season. A crushing victory over Whitehaven, one of the leading sides in the division, after putting out biggest rivals Castleford in the semi-final, was all the evidence anyone could need.

"I think it was really important. Early in the season we set our goals as wanting to do well in every competition.

"In the Challenge Cup we obviously weren't going to win it, but we put in a decent performance against Wigan.

"But with the Northern Rail Cup it was realistic and we had a really good chance in that. I felt as though the win will just give the lads a little bit of confidence knowing that if they get to a big stage at the back end of the year they know they can perform in a final.

"With all the build-up to it, the crowd and the media and all the hype, they reacted well to it."

With the level of performance being shown by the Vikings in advance of the game, McCormack had every faith in his side's ability.

"There is an advantage being full-time there's no doubt about that and sometimes you get games that you win a bit more comfortably than you think you're going to, but the test is getting that level of consistency. You don't want too big of a gap between your best performance and your worst performance.

"So far they have had that. Even when we played Halifax it wasn't a good performance but getting a bonus point and being in with a chance of winning it showed a certain determination.

"I expected us to win (the final) but I didn't expect us to win by that score. I thought we were clinical in everything that we did. I thought our forwards went really well and they had to do because Whitehaven, as we'll see this week are a good side. They are the best of the rest who aren't full-time."

He was impressed with the approach shown by the players in the build-up.

"The way they went about it, across the board, was superb. But I was really impressed with Mark Smith leading up to the game because being captain this season has been a bit different for Smithy. He's worked for some good captains, but when you're given the job yourself you don't know how you'll react.

"In the changing room before the game Mick Cassidy spoke really well from his experience of playing in finals.

"Dennis is normally pretty quiet, Toa's normally very quiet but Mick Cassidy and Smithy were excellent."

The feeling in the camp before the final was extremely positive and had been given some extra focus by the coaching team getting the players to return to the good habits they had displayed early in the season.

"Even though we'd had some games we won comfortably leading up to that Halifax game, we felt as though as a team we didn't stick to structures and it became a bit too individualised in some of the games.

"Even the Doncaster game where we ran up that big score, we fell away from our pattern a little bit and individually we went away from what we wanted to do.

"Just the little things, like when we scored we took it for granted and no one went up and congratulated each other.

"After the game we realised that. We did some edits after the scores at Doncaster and some of the other games compared to the early matches and that team spirit wasn't there. It was a kick up the backside."

McCormack stressed that these elements of team togetherness can make a big difference.

"It's little things that separate good teams from bad teams. Things like going onto the pitch together at warm up and leaving the field together at half-time. Sticking together when it's good times and bad times.

"When we had a good kick and good chase you couldn't see people encouraging their team-mates. We were taking it for granted. Since that Halifax game we've got that back."

With one piece of silverware already in the trophy cabinet, the focus is now very much on the end of season showpiece.

"We feel as though we've drawn a line under the first part of the season. We've won that competition and we're top of the league, but there's some massive games coming up for us now.

"The Monday we got back in, the first 10-15 minutes was talking about the final and how much they enjoyed it, but then the focus was back on National League and the games we've got coming up. Whitehaven, Dewsbury, Doncaster and Castleford.

"It's a massive end of the season with some difficult games."

How everyone else is playing and what the respective run-ins are like plays no part in his thinking, and freshening up the team is also on the agenda.

"I'm not bothered whatever anyone else is doing. Everyone is playing everyone else. If we win our games then no one else can touch us.

"I'm looking to strengthen as we speak. I have spoken to a Super League club about bringing in one more player. The board have backed us with it. It depends on how the Super

League games go. If they get injuries I might not be able to bring him here.

"Adam Sidlow and Martin Keavney are up at Workington and Adam has been great for them, he's been their stand out player and I wouldn't hesitate in bringing him back, but it's nice to bring in a new face and keep everyone on their toes."

The competition for places has been a significant change from the situation he faced in the previous season. But it isn't always easy leaving out players who haven't let the side down.

"It's totally different to last year. The team picked itself 99% of the time last year and if anyone played poorly they couldn't be dropped. It doesn't bear any relation at all to last year's situation.

"There are times when you have to leave someone like Andy Kirk or Gavin Dodd out who would probably get in any other team.

"It was a big call leaving Doddy out for the final. It was only about three weeks ago that he got the points scoring record but the reason was that Dean Gaskell has come in on probably four occasions and played really well and got man of the match awards and then I've dropped him. "He played that well against Dewsbury that I felt I couldn't do it again. He had a good game in the final as well.

"Andy Kirk has reacted probably the best way I've ever seen a professional react in that situation. I said to him I felt Toa was my starting centre and he took it. Andy has been in a situation at Wakefield where a couple of players were in front of him, but he's also been in the situation at Halifax where he was the starting centre, got injured and someone's come in had three or four great games, but Andy's come straight back in.

"Doddy took it well and wished the lads well. It's not pleasant telling people that you're not going to pick them, but there's not much you can do about it, I can only pick 17.

"I won't tell them lies, and I think that if I am honest with them about why the decisions have been made then they respect that."

Now those players have got to come good again for the end of the season and the play-off rounds which will determine whether the Vikings return to Super League. The coach, for one, can't wait.

"I'm really excited. At this stage of the season there will be some twists and turns. Teams like Halifax are starting to build up some momentum, these are the games you want to be involved in at the back end of the year.

"There's a lot of pressure on, but there's been pressure since last November when we got back into pre-season. I'm really looking forward to it."

17th July 2007   **Coach signs new contract**

Vikings fans received an unexpected boost following their cup final success when it was announced that Steve McCormack had signed a contract extension until the end of the 2009 season. Although the contract was signed some two weeks previously the news had been kept under wraps during the build up to Blackpool.

McCormack explained "To say the least I'm thrilled to be able to continue the work I've started here at Widnes. The start to this season has been great but we've still got a lot of work to do to become the finished article. One of my watchwords this season has been 'professionalism' and that has been evident from the players both during matches and at training. There are going to be a lot of changes in the sport over the next 12 – 18 months with the advent of a Super League Licensing system...... an important factor over this period is stability and I'm looking forward to playing my part in helping Widnes secure a franchise".

Delighted to secure the services of McCormack on an extended deal Widnes Chairman Peter Knowles added "When I took over as Chairman I saw it as a top priority to get Steve signed up as soon as possible. Steve has the respect from the players and all of the staff at the Vikings and has really turned this club around in the time he has been here. If we have a bright future at the club a large part of it is down to Steve".

Less than 12 months previously the coach was on the receiving end of irrational criticism but there was hardly a dissenting voice as fans realised this was a massive move to secure the future of the club, its drive towards Super League status, and a vital pre-cursor to the retention and recruitment of players for future seasons.

22nd July 2007 - NL1

| Widnes Vikings | 16 |
| Whitehaven | 14 |

Following the events in Blackpool everybody should have been aware that this was going to be a very different match indeed, and it had all the makings of an upset. The only similarity was the grey clouds hovering over the stadium, but in stark contrast to the previous week, by half-time the clouds matched the mood of the fans. Whilst not doubting the determination or dedication of the players it seemed that the whole squad had not 'come down' from the obvious 'high' of winning the Northern Rail Cup in such emphatic style, and were plainly off the pace for the majority of the afternoon. Far from taking a grip on the game, many players had difficulty getting a grip on the ball, as a string of handling errors constantly gave the initiative back to Whitehaven.

What became a very dull encounter had started reasonably brightly when, after ten minutes, Dennis Moran making his 300th career appearance, scored another typical interception try. With an apparent in-built ability to read the intentions of the opposition he calmly plucked the ball from the air and set off for the try line from inside his own half. Teasing the covering Broadbent with his change of pace he veered around the fullback to touch down under the posts and leave an easy conversion for Mick Nanyn.

Unlike last week the visitors did not cave in and instead took the fight to the Vikings, forcing some dogged defence deep into home territory. By half-time 'Haven had fought back sufficiently well to take a deserved lead of 8 - 6 into the dressing room thanks to a penalty and a converted try. Duffy's kicking was having a far greater effect on the game than last week, and when another deep effort was handled by Dean Gaskell on its way to touch the Cumbrians gained the field position that led to the try.

Worse was to come with the second half only four minutes old. With the defensive line formed high in their own half the Vikings failed to react when a chip over the top left Scott Grix marking three players and led to another converted try to extend the deficit to eight points. For the next thirty minutes the Widnes players worked hard to get back into the game, but to no avail. The crisp, inventive play that had been present all season was missing as the Vikings struggled to find a way through, round or over the Whitehaven defence. Again there seemed no prospect of a breakthrough as the ball was passed, and juggled, along the line in the 73rd minute until Bob Beswick hoisted a high kick that Jordan James knocked back to Ollie Wilkes. The prop lost control but the loose ball was flicked back to Moran who in turn put in a high kick to the wing for Damien Blanch to evade his marker and score in the corner as he was tackled. Nanyn missed with his attempt from the touchline, but became the hero only two minutes later. Trailing by just four points Widnes returned to the attack with new-found purpose and drive. A fine passing movement between Smith, Beswick and Scott Grix saw Nanyn running on to a fast flat pass from the fullback 20 metres out and he drove his powerful frame through the defence, and then turned towards the posts to make his conversion a formality.

Having struggled for the first seventy minutes the Vikings snatched victory from the jaws of defeat with an inspired last ten minutes, which drew the following comments from Steve McCormack: "I thought we were poor in most departments and we said at half time that the way we were playing we might have to wait until the last minute to win the game and so it turned out. Whitehaven were tremendous today; as good as we were bad. But it is an 80 minute game and I'm delighted with the victory."

Vikings: Grix, Blanch, Kohe-Love, Nanyn, Gaskell, Moran, Webster, Cassidy, Smith, Wilkes, Doran, Noone, Beswick. Subs: Summers, James, Kirk, Price

Tries: Moran, Blanch, Nanyn

Goals: Nanyn (2)

Whitehaven: Broadbent, Calvert, Eilbeck, Jackson(R), Maden, Joe, Duffy, Trindall, Mattinson, Fatialofa, Miller, Hill, Rudd. Subs: Sice, Seeds, Jackson(M), Wright

Tries: Jackson(M), Eilbeck

Goals: Rudd (3)

Referee: Mike Dawber.   Att: 3,299

NL1 Table

	P	W	D	L	B	F	A	Diff	Pts
Widnes	12	11	0	1	1	540	130	410	34
Castleford	12	11	0	1	0	560	171	389	33
Whitehaven	12	8	0	4	2	352	228	124	26
Halifax	12	7	0	5	1	366	277	89	22
Leigh	12	6	0	6	4	304	288	16	22
Dewsbury	12	4	0	8	5	254	347	-93	17
Sheffield	12	3	1	8	2	224	361	-137	13
Batley	12	3	1	8	1	240	455	-215	12
Rochdale	12	3	0	9	0	204	404	-200	9
Doncaster *	12	3	0	9	1	195	578	-383	4

• 6 points deducted for entering Administration

25ᵗʰ July 2007   **Disciplinary Hearing**

Following a hearing at Red Hall Bob Beswick was given a one match suspension and £100 fine for his part in joining a scuffle between Scott Grix and Whitehaven's Gary Broadbent in the Northern Rail Cup Final. Referee Jamie Leahy had placed the incident, which had resulted in Whitehaven's Gary Broadbent being sin-binned, on report. Following the hearing the following adjudication was announced:

> The Committee viewed the DVD and listened to explanations from player Beswick and his representative. The Committee stated that they could not allow this sort of behaviour on a rugby field where players think they can stand and trade punches. Whether this player was the

cause of the melee on the field does not matter. There was a deplorable melee where this player was involved throwing punches. The Committee took into account player Beswick's good disciplinary record, admission of misconduct but felt that this incident must be marked by a one match suspension and a £100 fine

27th July 2007   **Jigsaw complete ?**

The final piece of Steve McCormack's jigsaw fell into place when he boosted his squad for the run-in when Joel Tomkins joined the Vikings on an initial one month loan deal from Wigan Warriors. Announcing this deadline day signing McCormack said "It's a really good signing for the Club. Joel has tremendous ability and experience".

Having made his Wigan debut against Widnes in 2005, the 20 year-old Utility Forward, who had made 6 starts and 19 substitute appearances in Super League, immediately made his debut two days later against Doncaster.

29th July 2007 - NL1

Widnes Vikings	**40**
Doncaster	**18**

Former Vikings Senior Academy Coach John Stankevitch returned to the Halton Stadium with his new charges determined to cause an upset, and they put on a brave display knocking Widnes out of their stride with some effective, if not entertaining, rugby. Even allowing for the fact that the Vikings were disrupted by the absence of Mark Smith and Bob Beswick through injury and suspension respectively, positional changes, and Stankevitch's 'inside knowledge' of his former club, this was a distinctly below par performance.

Indeed it wasn't until Ollie Wilkes and Mick Cassidy were introduced to the action that the hosts appeared to have any real drive to their play. After a nervous and error strewn opening period the pair gained valuable ground which created the opportunity for Lee Doran to spin out of a tackle and force his way over the line in the 17th minute. Mick Nanyn's goal gave the Vikings full reward for Doran's third try of the campaign, but within two minutes Doncaster had levelled with their first real attacking move. It was approaching the half-hour mark before the Vikings could regain the lead when Nanyn, just inside his own half, took a long pass from Wilkes and set off on a powerful run to the line, brushing off challenges from Doncaster defenders. Ten minutes later another strong run from the in-form centre gave Doran the opportunity to stretch out in the tackle to plant the ball on the line. Having failed to convert his own try Nanyn duly extended the half-time lead to 16 - 6 with a straightforward kick.

Only two minutes into the second half Vikings' speedsters Dennis Moran and Damien Blanch combined in an 80 metre break but Blanch was thwarted as he was 'held up' by a resolute defence. Blanch was to gain revenge when just two minutes later he broke, centre-field, from his '40' to take on a depleted defence. Feinting to pass to the supporting Toa Kohe-Love on two occasions he finally touched down by the posts to give Nanyn an easy conversion.

Doncaster came charging back within six minutes when they easily burst through the home defence to reduce the deficit to ten points, before Widnes finally managed to create some daylight between the teams with two Kohe-Love tries either side of the hour mark. Using a combination of power and agility he forced his way through a crowded defence to score a brace of close range tries, on virtually the same blade of grass. With the relative comfort of an 18 point cushion Widnes cut loose with two eye-catching tries as they took the score to 40 - 12. On sixty seven minutes Wilkes set off on a typically forceful run some 30 metres out, and having broken through attempted tackles, had the determination, strength and speed to power on to the line.

The final Widnes try brought the biggest cheer of the afternoon when Nanyn and Ian Webster, deputising for the injured Smith, created the space for Gavin Dodd - no doubt fuelled by two weeks of frustration following his omission from the Cup Final team - to race in from half-way.

The final score of the afternoon, however, went to the visitors who underlined the transformation that Stankevitch had made since his appointment, and caused concern amongst the Widnes faithful as the 'business' end of the season approached. This erratic performance was hardly the ideal way to 'blood' loan signing Joel Tomkins, but having barely trained with his team-mates he showed some encouraging signs on his debut.

Admitting his disappointment with the performance Steve McCormack commented that: "We didn't reach the levels of recent weeks and all credit to Doncaster for that. It took some individual skill from the likes of Mick Nanyn, Damien Blanch, Gavin Dodd and Dennis Moran to give us the victory."

Vikings:	Grix, Blanch, Kohe-Love, Nanyn, Gaskell, Moran, Penny, James, Webster, Summers, Doran, Tomkins, Noone. Subs: Cassidy, Wilkes, Dodd, Price
Tries:	Doran (2), Nanyn, Blanch, Kohe-Love (2), Wilkes, Dodd
Goals:	Nanyn (4)

Doncaster:	Leaf, Skelton, Munro, Woods, Brown, For-ster, Gale, Hodgkinson, Richardson, Bur-gess, Lawton, Green, Benson. Subs: Buttery, Worrall, Anderson, Rowe.
Tries:	Burgess, Gale, Forster
Goals:	Gale (3)
Referee:	Thierry Alibert (Fra) Att: 2,607

2nd August 2007 - NL1

Leigh Centurions   0
Widnes Vikings   38

Appearing in front of the Sky Sports cameras for the seventh time this season the Vikings treated viewers to an exhibition of flowing rugby and clinical finishing. The stuttering perfor-mance of the previous week was forgotten as Mark Smith and Bob Beswick returned to mastermind a performance which saw Widnes put their hosts out of sight after just 25 minutes.

The Vikings were able to take up early residence in their opponents half, and Mick Nanyn duly converted a penalty, 35 metres out, in the third minute. As Leigh tried to reply Beswick collected a loose ball in the eighth minute to initiate an attack from his own 30 metre line, which produced drives from Dean Gaskell and Ollie Wilkes to return the Vikings to half-way where Smith shipped a pass to Dennis Moran. As the stand-off entered Leigh territory he had Joel Tomkins on his shoulder and the youngster took a short pass to stride home from 40 metres out. Nanyn missed the conversion but was soon to become the match-winner with a hat-trick of tries within the space of ten minutes as the Vikings turned the screw on their nemesis.

Nanyn's first try came in the 15th minute. Smith launched an attack deep in opposition territory with the ball passing through several pairs of hands to Moran whose high kick to the corner was fielded by Miles Greenwood, who then ran 'in goal' where he met the on-rushing Wilkes. The ball was dislodged on impact for Nanyn to simply place a hand on it to score near the posts and convert his own try to establish an early 12 point lead.

In the 22nd minute Scott Grix just foiled a 40/20 attempt on his 10 metre line, and set the Vikings on the attack again. A high tackle on Aaron Summers then saw the visitors advance to the Leigh 30 metre line where, from the re-start, Joel Penny and Paul Noone exchanged passes in centre-field before Penny passed wide to Nanyn. The centre dummied to pass outside to the supporting Gavin Dodd, shrugged off a couple of attempted tackles, and dived over the line, before adding the 'extras'.

Grix was again involved in the next try when, following a 25th minute break led by Jordan James and Dodd, he joined the line to play Gaskell in from 20 metres out. The winger was tackled just short of the line, but a swift passing movement saw the ball switched to the opposite wing via Grix, Moran, Noone, and Beswick for Nanyn to casually stroll in to complete his hat-trick and give the Vikings a 22 point lead.

The Widnes defence came under pressure for the remainder of the half and much of the second period, but the defence held firm and the lead was increased seven minutes after the break. After Moran had forced a knock-on 15 metres from the Leigh line the ball was switched inside only for Wilkes to be stopped just short. From the play-the-ball Smith fed Beswick who exchanged short passes with Noone before side-stepping the defence to register his 6th try of the season. Nanyn extended the lead to 28 - 0.

A period of concerted Leigh pressure followed as Widnes failed to launch a meaningful attack for ten minutes as they were penned into their own half. However, on the hour, the lead was further extended when another sweeping movement saw the ball transferred across the width of the pitch. Smith, Ian Webster, Moran, Toa Kohe-Love and Grix saw the ball into the hands of Gaskell who dived over.

The scoring was completed three minutes from time when Penny fielded a drop-out near half-way and set Dodd off on a run deep into the Leigh half. After Gareth Price had gained a further 10 metres Beswick slipped a pass to Grix whose side-step created the space for him to score against his old club.

Steve McCormack commented after the game that "the first half was as good as we have played all year…..we played at a pace we really want to be playing at every game". Of hat-trick hero Nanyn the coach said "he has made a fantastic contribution to our game play all season".

Vikings:	Grix, Gaskell, Kohe-Love, Nanyn, Dodd, Moran, Penny, Cassidy, Smith, Wilkes, Tomkins, Noone, Beswick. Subs:Summers, James, Webster, Price
Tries:	Tomkins, Nanyn (3), Beswick, Gaskell, Grix
Goals:	Nanyn (5)
Centurions:	Giles, Rivett, Couturier, Halliwell, Alstead, Greenwood, Hough, Wilson, McConnell, Stiles, Grundy, Taylor, Stewart. Subs: Butterworth, Pemberton, Cookson, Martins
Referee:	Gareth Hewer Att: 3,095

4ᵗʰ August 2007   **Museum opens**

Back in 2004 a chance conversation in the club shop led to a suggestion that the Super League fixture versus Bradford Bulls should be marketed as the 'First versus Current' World Club Champions. This in turn led to the realisation that the club's heritage was being under-played, and hence the idea of the museum was conceived.

Two and a half years later the hard work of Widnes Rugby League Heritage Group reaped its reward when the Widnes Vikings Rugby League Museum finally opened its doors to the public, following the official opening by David and Paul Hulme. The museum is now the proud guardian of in excess of 2000 items, in addition to a collection of more than 5000 match programmes.

From an initial 'starter' grant of £150, from Halton Borough Council in February 2005, the momentum and quality of the work being done led to total grant aid in excess of £63,000. Whilst £43,200 of that came from a successful bid to the Heritage Lottery Fund, the remainder came from a variety of local and regional bodies. In addition to the necessary financial support the museum also benefited from valuable assistance from former Vikings chairman Peter Knowles, the RFL and all Widnes supporters groups - in addition to practical advice from the curators of Liverpool FC Museum.

Underpinning the enthusiastic yet professional approach of the museum volunteers is the vocational training which they have undertaken as the museum works towards accreditation by the Museum, Libraries and Archives Council. This included such vital topics as Documentation, Inventories and the Handling, Cleaning and Care of objects.

With displays ranging from the Nat Silcock collection from the '20s and '30s through to the World Club Championship success of 1989 and on to the Northern Rail Cup victory of 2007, the result is an impressive collection of memorabilia, proficiently displayed and cared for. Not only did the museum meet with universal approval from all of the funding bodies at a special launch a few days earlier, it also created an impression on the hundreds of visitors that have since passed through its doors. Among those to have been impressed were Steve Mc-Cormack and those of his players who have witnessed the display of the club's former glories and heritage, with Widnes born players heard to say "I've got that at home" and "I was there"!

Not only does the museum offer the opportunity for supporters - and players - to catch up on their club's history, and view inspiring exhibits, it also provides a valuable extension to the work of the 'Vikings in the Community'. As well as the practical coaching of basic skills that is carried out in schools across the borough, the Museum affords them an insight into just how famous and successful their local club has been in the not so distant past, and how they can aspire to that success.

12th August 2007 - NL1

Widnes Vikings	**48**
Dewsbury Rams	**12**

Widnes went into this game knowing that victory would not only return them to the top of National league One - Castleford had won in midweek to leapfrog the Vikings - but also confirm their place in the 'top two' as the play-offs came into view.

They eventually ran out comfortable winners of an entertaining, end-to-end match spoilt only by some bewildering decisions from the man in the middle. For the fourth time this season a match at the Halton Stadium had been refereed by an overseas official, as the RFL seemingly used Widnes as a 'proving ground' for these referees.

With just three minutes on the clock a high tackle on Ollie Wilkes gave Mick Nanyn the opportunity to begin his 20-point haul for the day with a straightforward penalty. The first try of the afternoon came in the tenth minute when Toa Kohe-Love began a break inside his own half and progressed to the half-way line before giving a short pass inside to Damien Blanch. The flying winger showed a return to full fitness as he changed gear to pull away from the chasing defenders with some ease and touch down by the posts.

As in the earlier encounter, at the Tetley's Stadium, the Rams demonstrated their fighting spirit and took advantage of some slack defending to reduce the arrears to two points in the 18th minute. However the hosts immediately returned to the attack and just four minutes later Mark Smith and Bob Beswick combined to create the opening for Nanyn to burst over the line from 15 metres out. Failing to convert his own try was the only blemish on Nanyn's performance.

In the run up to half-time the Vikings ran in two more tries, both scored by the impressive Joel Penny, and had a third disallowed. On the half-hour Penny took advantage of a penalty inside the 10 metre line to jink his way through a static defence to score under the posts, before Dean Gaskell was extremely unfortunate to have a try ruled out for an alleged forward pass as he got on the end of an excellent passing movement. Then, as the hooter sounded Blanch and Scott Grix kept the ball alive as it was worked left for Paul Noone and Nanyn to link up before releasing Penny to sprint for the line from 20 metres out. The Vikings went in at the break with a comfortable 24 - 6 lead.

To bring everybody back down to earth the visitors scored

a try just four minutes after the break, but despite some enterprising play did not trouble the scorers again, as the Vikings went on to double their first half score. Widnes again demonstrated their ability to raise their game as mid-way through the half they scored twice within two minutes. First Paul Noone was the beneficiary of sterling work from Mick Cassidy that set Penny off on another run towards the line before off-loading to the supporting Noone under the posts. Then for the second time in the match Blanch demonstrated his pace and agility by running half the length of the pitch, with his marker not knowing which way to turn, to score under the posts.

The Rams continued to play their part but in the 68th minute the Vikings' lead was further extended by Gavin Dodd when he was put through following a smart interception by Jordan James. The fullback showed pace equal to Blanch as he went on a mazy run to the line to underline his returning form and confidence. On a day of some amazing passing and movement, at pace, Kohe-Love rounded off such a move to score the final try with a minute to go.

Nanyn's return of eight goals and 20 points left him one goal short of the Club's season's best total of 140, and just 14 points short of his own Club record mark of 388 in 2006.

Claiming that his team's play "was either fantastic or ordinary" Steve McCormack declared that this inconsistency was something "which we need to work on".

Vikings:	Dodd, Blanch, Kohe-Love, Gaskell, Grix, Penny, Cassidy, Smith, Wilkes, Tomkins, Noone, Beswick. Subs: Summers, James, Webster, Doran
Tries:	Blanch (2), Nanyn, Penny (2), Noone, Dodd, Kohe-Love
Goals:	Nanyn (8)

Rams: Preece, Powell, Hall, Crouthers, Buchanan, Walker, Lawford, Hobson, Finn, Maloney, Robinson, Bretherton, Weeden. Subs: Haigh, Kelly, Helme, Crawley

Tries: Robinson, Crouthers

Goals: Finn, Lawford

Referee: Leon Williamson (NZ)   Att: 2,853

NL1 Table

	P	W	D	L	B	F	A	Diff	Pts
Widnes	15	14	0	1	1	666	160	506	43
Castleford	15	14	0	1	0	668	219	449	42
Whitehaven	15	10	0	5	3	414	282	132	33
Halifax	15	9	0	6	2	492	361	131	29
Leigh	15	7	0	8	4	368	398	-30	25
Sheffield	15	5	1	9	2	362	473	-111	19
Dewsbury	15	4	0	11	6	312	469	-157	18
Batley	15	4	1	10	2	304	547	-243	16
Rochdale	15	3	0	12	1	274	536	-262	10
Doncaster *	15	4	0	11	1	259	674	-415	7

* 6 points deducted for entering Administration

Loan deal

Another young prospect, Rob Draper, left the Halton Stadium

to spend the next month on loan at Swinton Lions. Expected by many to push for a regular first team spot, Rob had been hampered by injury.

16th August 2007 - NL1

Widnes Vikings   18
Castleford Tigers   24

The Vikings fell to their first home defeat in the league against their nearest rivals in NL1, and as the play-offs approached, lost the advantage of pole position in the process. There can be little doubt that the visitors took their chances better than their hosts, and in that sense were the better team, but this sense of reality was lost amongst the fury felt by fans about the performance of the referee, which at best could be described as idiosyncratic. The official constantly mystified the home crowd with his decisions, and 'non-decisions', throughout the game, and was left in no doubt about his popularity as he left the pitch at the end of the match! However the reality was that the Vikings were collectively 'off the boil' and now faced the prospect of returning to The Jungle for the Qualifying Semi-Final.

It had all started so promisingly when Widnes took a 5th minute lead through Mick Nanyn. Toa Kohe-Love had pounced on a loose ball on his own 10 metre line which allowed Scott Grix and Dean Gaskell to carry the Vikings to half-way for Joel Penny to kick deep into Tigers' territory. Damien Blanch then took advantage of another fumble to drive to within two metres of the line. Quick hands from Mark Smith, Bob Beswick and Grix promptly isolated eight defenders as the ball was rapidly swept wide for Nanyn to stroll in from 10 metres out, but failing to add the conversion. For the next twenty minutes of end to end rugby the Vikings were more than a match for their opponents but failed to turn their possession into points, and were to ultimately pay the penalty.

Castleford took the lead with a converted penalty in the 27th minute when Williams eluded Dennis Moran in the corner to dive onto a grubber from Brough, who had come out of his shell after two poor matches against the Vikings earlier in the season. Four minutes later Brough scored from one of a string of penalties awarded against the Vikings. In their next attack the visitors forced a goal line drop out from which they immediately drove back into home territory before the ball was switched wide for Wainwright to score in the corner. The momentum was now fully with the visitors but the Vikings dug deep in the final minutes of the half, and got their reward in the 39th minute. From a rare penalty awarded in Widnes' favour Mick Cassidy and Ollie Wilkes reached half-way before a typical passing movement ended with Moran being stopped just short of the line. From the play-the-ball Kohe-Love dived over from a couple of yards for his 17th try of the season. Nanyn converted to reduce the arrears to six points at half-time.

Having regained a toe-hold in the game Widnes were dealt a blow within a minute of the re-start when Moran was sin-binned for a late challenge on Brough, who also converted the penalty. However Nanyn again reduced the arrears in the 45th minute when he kicked a penalty from 35 metres, equalling Mick Burke's record of 140 goals in season 1978/79.

Castleford extended their lead again in the 52nd minute as a result of what seemed yet another contentious penalty. With a Castleford player laying motionless in front of him Smith moved away, less than a metre, to resume play. In awarding the penalty the exaggerated signal of the referee implied that Smith was seeking to gain an unfair advantage. The visitors were immediately back on the attack and when Dean Gaskell shot off his line prematurely Dixon cut through the gap despite a desperate lunge by Nanyn.

Unlike the first half the Vikings seemed unable to find the spark to fight back, and were dealt a further blow on the hour when another penalty saw the Tigers cement a 24 - 12 lead. However in the 65th minute they drew strength when Blanch was held up in the corner and finally put the visitors under some pressure, which led to Higgins being sin-binned in the 71st minute. Shortly after this Gavin Dodd was also adjudged to have been held up in the corner after taking a smart pass from Beswick to sprint in from 18 metres out. In the next attack Nanyn collected the ball, on his wing, 40 metres out and barged his way in-field to gain ground before off-loading to Smith whose impudent 'back-door' pass allowed Moran to put in a grubber to the corner. Blanch was just beaten to the ball by a soccer-style sliding tackle. As Widnes continued to build pressure Nanyn was the next to be 'held-up', in the 75th minute, before a passage of play saw the ball move left, right and then back to the left where Nanyn off-loaded to Kohe-Love who put Dodd in from five metres. Nanyn's conversion made the score 18 - 24 with less than five minutes remaining. With time running out there was still time for the big centre to break and feed Dodd on half-way only for the referee to call a forward pass as the winger raced clear.

Taking defeat on the chin Steve McCormack remained upbeat as he said "There are still two games left in the league and we know that ourselves and Cas will meet again before the Grand Final. We have already won at The Jungle and if the play-offs see us travel back there, it holds no fears."

Vikings: Grix, Blanch, Kohe-Love, Nanyn, Gaskell, Moran, Penny, Cassidy, Smith, Wilkes, Doran, Noone, Beswick. Subs: Summers, James, Webster, Dodd

| Tries: | Nanyn, Kohe-Love, Dodd |
| Goals: | Nanyn (3) |

Tigers:	Donlan, Williams, Shenton, Dixon, Wainwright, Thackeray, Brough, Higgins, Henderson, Leafa, Guttenbeil, Charles, Clayton. Subs: Westerman, Boyle, Glassie, Lupton
Tries:	Williams, Wainwright, Dixon
Goals:	Brough (6)

| Referee: | Ashley Klein | Att: 4,598 |

17th August 2007   **More experience**

Adam Bowman joined Swinton Lions on a month's loan in another bid by the club to get valuable, competitive experience for its young prospects. Bowman, who made his senior debut last season joined fellow Viking Rob Draper at Sedgley Park as the Lions qualified for the NL2 play-offs.

2nd September 2007 - NL1

| **Whitehaven** | 18 |
| **Widnes Vikings** | 22 |

The Vikings returned to action after a break of seventeen days, against their Northern Rail Cup Final opponents at the Recreation Ground, in a bid to get their promotion push back on track. Having witnessed Joel Penny limping out of the Halton Stadium with ice packs on each ankle after the Castleford match it was reassuring to see him take his place in the starting line-up. At first a repeat of the Cup Final performance seemed on the cards as Widnes raced into a ten point lead after just five minutes, but by the final whistle they had to thank an excellent defensive display for securing a narrow victory. The visitors controlled the first half without firing on all cylinders, but played second fiddle to their hosts in the second period as they were limited to only occasional excursions into 'Haven territory.

The Vikings made their breakthrough in the 3rd minute with a move started and finished by Scott Grix. Having fielded a high punt under pressure the fullback released Gavin Dodd to make a 20 metre beak from his 10 metre line, before the winger's neat pass in turn allowed Dennis Moran to surge 40 metres deep into the opposition half. Moran toyed with the two remaining defenders as he waited for support, which came as Grix caught up with play to score by the posts. Mick Nanyn duly added his first conversion of the afternoon.

A high tackle on Ollie Wilkes, straight from the re-start, gave Widnes possession on the half-way line. Play progressed to within 25 metres of the Whitehaven line before Mark Smith fed Moran who delivered a delightful chip which hung in the air for Damien Blanch to gather at speed to touch down in the corner. In a purple patch for the Vikings the winger almost converted a pass from Toa Kohe-Love, but was ushered into touch by the defence. The hosts reduced the arrears minutes later when the Vikings' defence was sucked in-field to allow Maden to score a converted try.

Nanyn edged the Vikings' further ahead when he converted a penalty under the posts, before he claimed an 'assist' in the last score of the half. Awarded another penalty on their '40' Penny took a quick tap to dart 15 metres before the ball was switched right to Moran, who came back in-field to fire a pass to Nanyn who in turn put Dodd in from 10 metres out. Nanyn missed the conversion as the visitors went in at the break leading 16 - 6. Shortly after the break 'Haven again reduced the arrears after a series of handling errors allowed Rudd to make ground to score despite the attentions of four Widnes defenders on the line. Widnes' last contribution came in the 49th minute, when drives by Aaron Summers (twice) and Blanch saw them advance before Bob Beswick's grubber into the corner caused confusion in the Whitehaven defence. Maden appeared to be in several minds as to how to deal with the bouncing ball, and as he over-ran it Dodd simply grounded the ball to register his 200th point in Widnes colours. Nanyn's conversion took the score to 22 - 12, and his own tally for the season to 390, thus surpassing the club record he had set in 2006.

From this point on Whitehaven dominated the match and reduced the Widnes advantage to a nervous four points in the 55th minute. Moving deep into Widnes territory on the back of a penalty the visitors' right wing was exposed, as the defence was again drawn in-field, allowing the hosts to notch a converted try.

The referee had issued several warnings to the Whitehaven captain about continued infringements and finally lost his patience after 65 minutes when he sin-binned Fletcher. Before the Vikings could take advantage of their numerical advantage matters had been evened up as Summers also took a ten minute rest. Worse was to come as the Vikings had a spell with just 11 players on the pitch as Beswick was 'binned' for what appeared an accidental collision with an opponent whilst attempting to charge down the ball. After appearing to be sprinting for the finish line in the 5th minute the Vikings finally crawled over the line thanks to an outstanding second half defensive effort as the inability to complete sets had piled constant pressure on the visitors.

Steve McCormack commented after the game that "It was an ugly win but it was a win. Any victory here is a good win and the players had to work extremely hard for the points. We didn't play particularly well but the effort was there. The players are tired now but it was good tackling practice for the play-offs."

Vikings:	Grix, Blanch, Kohe-Love, Nanyn, Dodd, Moran, Penny, Summers, Smith, Wilkes, Tomkins, Noone, Beswick. Subs: Cassidy, James, Webster, Doran
Tries:	Grix, Dodd (2), Blanch
Goals:	Nanyn (3)

Whitehaven:	Broadbent, Calvert, Seeds, Jackson, Maden, Joe, Rudd, Trindall, Smith, Fatialofa, Baldwin, Fletcher, McAvoy. Subs: Sice, Hill, Jackson, Wright
Tries:	Maden, Rudd, Calvert
Goals:	Rudd (3)

Referee:	Peter Taberner	Att: 2,360

9th September 2007 - NL1

Batley Bulldogs	18
Widnes Vikings	34

It was no secret that fans had been expressing concern in recent weeks about the apparent loss of individual and collective form and flair as the 'business end' of the season approached.

As Steve McCormack plotted the route to a possible Grand Final his selection was hampered by minor injuries to Toa Kohe-Love and Dennis Moran. The decision to give Ian Webster and Gareth Price the benefit of 80 minutes rugby with the Senior Academy added to the changes as Dean Gaskell was recalled with Gavin Dodd moving to fullback and Scott Grix to stand-off. Promising youngster Richard Myler, having been involved with the squad for recent games, finally made his debut from the bench.

Kicking off, against an enthusiastic Batley team, with the benefit of the steep Mount Pleasant slope, the Vikings again failed to impress, although they were ultimately too strong for their hosts. After Joel Penny had a try mysteriously disallowed it was the Bulldogs who opened the scoring. Moving the ball around with ease, they broke the Widnes defensive line in the 10th minute to score in the corner, as the wing was again left unprotected. But as had happened many times this season the Vikings showed their resolve and fought back to equalise within three minutes. Pushing down the hill from the re-start the Vikings won a penalty 15 metres out. The ball passed quickly between Mark Smith, Penny and Paul Noone before Smith slung a long ball out to Mick Nanyn for the centre to barge his way over the line to level matters.

The next ten minutes were spent camped out in the Batley half without creating any clear-cut opportunities, until in the 23rd minute the Vikings capitalised on an untidy piece of play. A pass from Smith dropped at the feet of Grix but eluded both him and his marker to bounce through to Joel Tomkins to collect and score his second try in Vikings' colours, with Nanyn's conversion finally easing Widnes into a six point lead. From the kick-off the Vikings immediately charged forward for Bob Beswick to break from inside his own half, attack the heart of the Bulldogs defence before passing to Penny to allow the scrum-half to score under the posts. Nanyn's conversion gave the visitors a 16 - 4 advantage at half-time, but their possession should have yielded a greater reward.

As if to underline this just two minutes after the break Batley again scored out wide to reduce the arrears to eight points. The Vikings rallied again, in the 50th minute when Beswick was first to react to a loose ball. As the ball came loose from a five-man tackle the loose forward collected the ball and set off into home territory, rolling two tackles before off-loading to the supporting Nanyn. The centre set off on a 30 metre run, and while fighting to maintain his balance played a hopeful ball inside which was eventually gathered by Lee Doran who strolled through the defence to score unchallenged by the posts. Six minutes later, having gained possession and advanced up the hill to the Batley '20' the ball was switched between Beswick, Penny and Grix for the latter to put Andy Kirk through with a long pass to the wing, only for the centre to be stopped two metres short of the line. From the play-the-ball Grix put in a grubber which bounced kindly for Ollie Wilkes to gather and touch down before Nanyn's conversion took the score to 28 - 8. The lead was further extended minutes later when following a Widnes scrum Aaron Summers was also stopped just short of the line. From the play-the-ball Smith played the ball back to Penny on the 10 metre line, who looking more like his creative self, jinked his way past several defenders to score his tenth try since signing for the Vikings. Widnes then seemed to ease off and the Bulldogs ran in two late tries, the second of which came as the defence seemed to switch off between the hooter and the final whistle.

With the score at 34 - 8 McCormack took the opportunity to 'blood' Myler, who responded by showing glimpses of the ability that had earned him his call-up to the senior squad.

The coach admitted disappointment with the performance,

adding that "Batley played really well but we contributed to that with some poor defence and a lack of flair on attack."

Bulldogs:	Stokes; Lindasy, Farrell, Langley, Marns; Toohey, Colley; Jarrett, Lythe, Stenchion, Gallagher, Spears, Paterson Subs: Barlow, Lingard, Thewliss, Simpson
Tries:	Farrell, Lingard, Lindsay, Paterson
Goal:	Farrell
Vikings:	Dodd, Blanch, Kirk, Nanyn, Gaskell, Grix, Penny, Summers, Smith, Wilkes, Tomkins, Noone, Beswick. Subs: Cassidy, James, Myler, Doran
Tries:	Nanyn, Tomkins, Penny (2), Doran, Wilkes
Goals:	Nanyn (5)
Referee:	Mike Dawber Att: 1,139

NL1 Table

	P	W	D	L	B	F	A	Diff	Pts
Castleford	18	17	0	1	0	860	247	613	51
Widnes	18	16	0	2	2	740	220	520	50
Halifax	18	12	0	6	2	616	421	195	38
Whitehaven	18	11	0	7	5	474	342	132	38
Leigh	18	9	0	9	4	454	474	-20	31
Sheffield	18	6	1	11	4	414	527	-113	24
Dewsbury	18	5	0	13	6	346	572	-226	21

Batley	18	5	1	12	2	372	645	-273	19
Rochdale	18	3	0	15	1	302	700	-398	10
Doncaster *	18	5	0	13	1	348	778	-430	10

* 6 points deducted for entering Administration

Bonus Point review

Much discussion had taken place pre-season, amongst supporters of National League clubs, about the introduction of the new points system for National League competitions for 2007. Opinion quickly became polarised between the extremes of 'great incentive' and 'devaluing winning', but the one certainty was that we would have to wait and see.

Analysing the competitions in which Widnes competed the reality is that if the 'tables' were re-calculated under the old system (2 points for a win and 1 point for a draw) there would be no significant difference, and certainly no effect on the promotion and relegation issues.

In the NRC Group 6 competition Leigh gained two bonus points, but this didn't enable them to 'leapfrog' any other team. The final positions in the four team - 12 match - group were identical under either system.

Greater variation may have been expected within National League One - a competition totalling 90 matches - but even here there was minimal effect on the final outcome. Taking account of Doncaster's points deduction for entering Administration, the only change to the final league table would have been Dewsbury (6 bp - 7th) and Batley (2 bp - 8th) swapping places under the old system. If Doncaster had not suffered a points penalty from the RFL they would have finished in ninth position under either points system.

In an ironic twist there were 31 matches in NL1 in 2006 in which the winning margin was 12 points or less, whilst in 2007 the actual number of bonus points awarded was 27. On that basis the change failed to meet its target of increasing the number of close-fought encounters. This only leaves the subjective view of whether matches were made more entertaining by 'losing' teams chasing an extra point, or whether the system rewarded the dour, hard-to-beat teams.

13th September 2007   **Coach 'on-line'**

Steve McCormack took part in a live 'web-chat' courtesy of the Widnes World, with fans putting questions on a range of topics to the Vikings coach.

Naturally many questions centred on the likelihood, and consequences of promotion to Super League, with McCormack reaffirming the club's desire to return to the top flight this year, with the longer term ambition to be "an established Super League club with many youngsters who have come through the academy ranks playing regular first grade." Whilst conceding that "the promoted team will be behind every other team in Super League with regards to recruitment" - due to the timing of the National League Grand Final - he was confident of landing some bargains if the club claimed victory in the Grand Final. "We have a few players signed up for Super League contracts and have had some players both here and abroad who have agreed to come. It's just a case of us going up." He also paid tribute to the current playing staff by adding "there is a number of our current squad who could comfortably make the step up to Super League" adding that "some real promising players have come through the ranks this year, even though they've had limited first team experience. We know if given the opportunity they can step up."

In answer to a question about Dennis Moran's ability to tackle 'above his weight' the coach felt his stand-off had been "excellent defensively… and it inspires other players."

Other answers attributed to the Vikings supremo ranged from the serious ……

"This year our defensive effort has been outstanding. We have finished the regular season with the best defensive record in the division. We are also aware that big improvements in all areas need to happen over the next few weeks."

"Stanky was a big part of our back room staff but I fully encouraged him to take up the post at Doncaster. There are not many Head Coach's jobs available and when you get the opportunity you have to grab it with both hands. I'm sure he will be a great success at Doncaster."

"A couple of weeks ago, I spent Saturday morning walking around the Vikings Heritage Museum and it made me realise what great history the club has got. It is everybody's intention connected with the club to get the club back into the top division and create some history for ourselves."

to the not so serious…….

"Can you send that email (*about his Wigan roots*) again in 15 minutes. I can't answer it at the moment, as I am just tucking in to my meat and potato pie and I'm frightened of it going onto my shell suit."

"I gave it (*Cup Final Suit*) back to Rab C Nesbitt after the game."

14th September 2007   'Player of the Year Awards'

This was the Vikings Supporters Club's third highly successful event of the year, held in a packed Bridge Suite, and again superbly MC'd by Mark Naughton and Gary McGrath. With the mood naturally buoyed by the team's on-field successes, and many of the senior squad spread around 'supporters tables' the players were even more accessible to their admiring fans. The evening was described by many as the "best yet" and a fitting reward for the hard work put in over the years by Alan, Denise, Gordon, Marie, Mark, Maurice, Noreen, Sandra and Tracey organising such events that had resulted in a another excellent year of fund raising.

The awards were as follows:

Junior Academy

Player of the Year	Dave Haughton
Runner-up	Shane Grady
Third	Richard Myler

Senior Academy

Player of the Year	Mike Morrison
Runner-up	Paddy Flynn
Third	Paul Crook

First Team

Player of the Year	Dennis Moran
Runner-up	Oliver Wilkes
Third	Scott Grix

Players' Player of the Year	Dennis Moran

A special presentation was also made to Mick Nanyn to recognise his outstanding achievements in 2007. Not only did Nanyn set a new record of 161 for the most goals in a season, previously held by Mick Burke (140), he also extended his own points in a season record to 434.

To round off the evening on a light-hearted note the following 'unofficial awards' were made by Mark Naughton:

Extreme Makeover Award
Steve McCormack was the proud(?) recipient of this award. As Mark said, "it was OUT with the shell-suits, and IN with the *FARAH* trousers, *MATALAN* shirts, and *LEATHER-LOOK* brogues – for this man in 2007!"

Bare-Faced Cheek(s) Award
Aaron Summers collected this award "for his wonderful choice in underwear, especially his little red number that he wore on matchdays – proving to one and all, that he was always up for the CRACK!"

Best Dressed Australian Award
Unfortunately this award was withheld as in the words of our host "none of our overseas players met the criteria"!

CHAPTER SIX

Extra Time

As the play-offs approached the euphoria and confidence built up amongst fans during the season seemed to have almost completely dissipated. Perhaps this was understandable as performances on the pitch seemed to have also lost their confidence and swagger. As the Sky commentators pointed out back in July, no team winning the Northern Rail Cup, since the Final moved to Bloomfield Road, had gone on to success in the National League Grand Final. As the performances dipped from the peak established in Blackpool there seemed to be an unspoken resignation that the 'Cup' was going to be our lot for 2007, and the search for scapegoats began!

Doubt was suddenly cast on the desire, and ability, of the very players that had lifted the Cup and taken the Vikings to within touching distance of the holy grail - Super League status. True, the performances over the final few matches had become more workmanlike than inspiring, but this hardly justified the sudden appearance of white flags being waved in the direction of West Yorkshire.

Since the defeat at home to Castleford it had been an uphill struggle to reclaim top spot in NL1 and so it was that the

Qualifying Semi-Final took place at The Jungle. Yet again the Widnes faithful demonstrated their loyalty to the cause, with another mid-week exodus along the M62, and showed the powers-that-be the commitment and passion that they would bring to Super League.

20th September 2007 - NL1 Qualifying Semi-Final

Castleford Tigers	**26**
Widnes Vikings	**8**

Steve McCormack was initially able to name a full-strength squad for the visit to The Jungle as he attempted to qualify for the Grand Final at the first attempt. However by kick-off he had lost the services of the influential Joel Penny, with Ian Webster coming in at scrum-half.

In a match played throughout at an electric pace the Vikings, having opened the scoring in the 8th minute were not bettered by their hosts until the hour mark. Castleford roared 'out of the gates' from the kick-off leading to some early defensive work for the Vikings, but the visitors gained a penalty, 10 metres out, when the ball was 'stripped' from Ollie Wilkes with four players in the tackle. Mick Nanyn duly scored from in front of the posts to ease Widnes nerves on and off the pitch.

Building pressure through three successive 'sets' Widnes crossed the Castleford try line twice within the space of 30 seconds in the 14th minute, but failed to trouble the scorers on either occasion. First Nanyn collected an errant pass from Bob Beswick 15 metres out, turned and attacked the line only to be held up 'in goal' by the four defenders he had dragged with him. From the re-start play was immediately switched to the right wing where Damien Blanch touched down only for the score to be wiped out for a forward pass by Toa Kohe -Love. The relentless pace continued as play switched from end to end with defences on top, until in the 27th minute the Tigers conceded another penalty, just 15 metres out for a high tackle on Scott Grix. Nanyn's second goal gave the Vikings a slender 4- 0 advantage. Despite their barnstorming start and some excellent kicking the hosts had not seriously threatened the Widnes line but opened their account after thirty two minutes through a dubious penalty. As play was switched back inside Mark Smith and Paul Noone tackled Donlan just 10 metres out in centre-field. As the fullback went to ground he appeared to throw his feet in the air and the referee gave the penalty for dangerous play. Just four minutes later the scores were level when Lee Doran was penalised for a clumsy rather malicious high tackle.

The travelling support, and the television viewers back in Widnes would have been happy that the Vikings had seemingly repelled the best that Castleford could offer, and could, maybe should, have been in front.

The second half began at the same high tempo as the first with both teams attacking at pace. The first try of the match came in the 47th minute as Widnes re-established their four point lead. As a result of yet another strong challenge from Kohe-Love Castleford knocked-on wide on their 30 metre line. From the re-start the ball was moved quickly along the line to Nanyn wide on the left who drove his large frame past five defenders to register his 27th try of the season. There could certainly be no doubting the desire in the camp as the centre disappeared under a 'pile on' of team-mates. The conversion attempt shaved the outside of the post from a difficult position by the touchline.

However in the 54th minute Nanyn went from hero to villain as the Tigers capitalised on a rare mistake from the big man. Facing his own line some fifteen metres out the centre attempted to pass the ball back to Gavin Dodd, but Wainwright came up on his blindside to intercept and sprint for the line, touching down under the posts. TV analysis later indicated that the video referee - Ashley Klein - had overlooked a knock-on by Castleford in the build up. Within minutes the Vikings had spurned a chance to re-take the lead when Kohe-Love dropped a pass from Dennis Moran just two metres short. This missed opportunity proved to be the turning point in the game as, courtesy of a harsh decision against Mick Cassidy on half-way, the Tigers moved downfield to score the first of three tries in an eight minute period to clinch their place in the Grand Final.

Disappointed at again having to take the long route to the Grand Final McCormack said "In the first half I think both sides were exceptional. But we made a couple of little errors and gave up some field position, so congratulations to them. We'll need to turn up next week with the same attitude but we'll need to play a little bit better."

Tigers:	Donlan, Wainwright, Dixon, Shenton, Williams, Thackeray, Brough, Higgins, Henderson, Clayton, Guttenbeil, Westerman, Lupton. Subs: McGoldrick, Charles, Boyle, Leafa
Tries:	Wainwright, Williams, Westerman (2)
Goals:	Brough (5)
Vikings:	Grix, Blanch, Kohe-Love, Nanyn, Dodd,Moran, Webster, Summers, Smith, Wilkes, Tomkins, Noone, Beswick. Subs: Cassidy, James, Myler, Doran

Try: Nanyn

Goals: Nanyn (2)

Referee: Richard Silverwood   Att: 6,179

26th April 2007 - NL1   Elimination Semi-Final

Widnes Vikings   36
Halifax   24

Reflecting on the defeat at Castleford in his programme notes Steve McCormack said "The players were sombre after the game and rightly so. They were all disappointed at the result, and that is a sign of a good group of players. Throughout 2007 we have never settled for second best and it is vital that we bounce back tonight. I have every confidence in the players and I'm sure they have put Thursday's defeat behind them."

As the Vikings prepared to take their second chance at qualification for the Grand Final it was announced that in-form prop Aaron Summers had not recovered from a calf injury picked up at Castleford, but on a positive note Joel Penny was passed fit to return. Summers' place in the 18-man squad was taken by Senior Academy Player of the Year Mike Morrison, whose last senior appearance was in the Challenge Cup-tie against Wigan Warriors back in April. Workington's elimination from the NL2 play-offs allowed Adam Sidlow to return to the Halton Stadium and claim a place on the bench.

An air of nervous anticipation filled the ground as the crowd built slowly towards kick-off, with the small, but vocal, band of Halifax supporters playing their part. Mark Naughton brought a new edge to the match-day experience as he whipped the home fans into a state of raucous animation not witnessed for some time. Virtually the whole stadium rose as one to greet Mark Smith and his men with a deafening roar as the players took the field for the final home game of this exciting season.

The Vikings dominated early possession, preventing the visitors from threatening their line, but had to wait until the 11th minute to take the lead through a penalty converted from 22 metres by the trusty boot of Mick Nanyn. The lead was short-lived as in the 14th minute Halifax moved to the Widnes '30' on the back of a penalty awarded against Mick Cassidy. This first meaningful venture into Widnes territory ultimately saw the visitors touch down in the corner to silence the home fans.

Continuing the tactic adopted at Castleford the Vikings again 'kicked' their next penalty although only 10 metres out, to level matters in the 17th minute. The kicking game, much criticised at Castleford, was far more effective this time out as Halifax were constantly pushed deep into their own half as the hosts established territorial advantage. This pressure paid off in the 26th minute when Paul Noone scored his 20th career try. Damien Blanch, Jordan James and Adam Sidlow advanced downfield before Smith and Joel Penny saw the ball to Scott Grix who immediately released Nanyn on a diagonal run from 30 metres out. The centre then passed inside for Noone to see the ball home.

Despite constant pressure it was not until four minutes from the break that the Vikings extended their lead. The re-surgent Grix read the bounce of a high kick to gather cleanly on his 10 metre line, sidestep a challenge and sprint 70 metres down the left wing before being halted. In the next tackle Halifax conceded a penalty for offside 18 metres out in cen-tre-field and Nanyn's kick saw the home side into the dressing room with a lead of 12 - 4, although this did not reflect the amount of possession they had enjoyed.

Halifax immediately went on the attack as the second period opened but five minutes into the half a typical Dennis Moran interception set up Smith for his first points since the Northern Rail Cup Final. As he defended deep in his own half the ball was drawn to Moran's outstretched hand and he set off with Blanch and Smith in close support. With the defence trailing he passed inside for Smith to score under the posts. Five minutes later the contest appeared to be over when, following interplay between Bob Beswick and Penny, Grix set off from his 30 metre line and as he approached the opposition '30' fed Smith who outpaced the covering defenders. We were now witnessing the flowing rugby that had gained so many admirers earlier in the season but in the 61st minute the pacy Penkywicz caught the Widnes defence on the back foot to set up a try for Royston to reduce the arrears.

The Vikings reacted positively to this reverse but were fortunate to escape when Halifax knocked-on with the line at their mercy, giving the home side the opportunity to move to within five metres of the Halifax line. From the play-the-ball the ball moved smartly from Ian Webster to Smith and on to the Halifax-born Grix whose footwork took him past three defenders to score, in the 65th minute, from 20 metres out. The conversion took the score to 30 - 10 but with only 15 minutes remaining uncharacteristically sloppy Widnes defence on their line allowed Watene to place a hand on a loose ball to keep Halifax interested. Worse was to come as straight from the re-start the visitors went the length of the field to score - albeit from a blatant forward pass - to set nerves jangling among the home supporters.

In a match that ebbed and flowed from almost first to last Widnes were next to score, in the 77th minute, with a move started and finished by Beswick. The loose forward was first to react to a loose ball and regain possession on his own '40'. The ball was then moved upfield for Oliver Wilkes to off-load to Smith who in turn set Beswick off on a mazy run from 30 metres out to score by the posts. Nanyn's eighth goal from eight attempts on the night was also his 160th of the season. Even though they had finally clinched a trip to Leeds and a place in the Grand Final, the Vikings were still to be hit again as Halifax scored in the final minute.

Several players who had been below par over the last few weeks displayed a timely return to form, none more so than Grix who produced a man-of-the-match performance after admitting that against Castleford he was so "pumped up" that he had tried "to do four men's jobs rather than concentrate on my own." Steve McCormack said "I had put Scott under a bit of pressure during the week and he responded very well," adding that "it doesn't matter if you go through at the first or second attempt as long as you go through. There is not a lot between ourselves and Castleford and the pressure is on both teams."

Vikings:	Grix, Blanch, Kohe-Love, Nanyn, Dodd, Moran, Penny, Cassisdy, Smith, Wilkes, Tomkins, Noone, Beswick. Subs: Webster, James, Sidlow, Doran
Tries:	Noone, Smith (2), Grix, Beswick
Goals:	Nanyn (8)
Halifax:	Royston, Gibson, Roberts, Varkulis, Greenwood, Holroyd, Watson, Southern, Penkywicz, Wrench, Larder, Smith (P), Joseph. Subs: Hoare, Ball, Trinder, Watene

Tries: Roberts, Royston, Watene, Varkulis, Hoare

Goals: Holroyd (2)

Referee: Phil Bentham   Att: 3,347

2nd October 2007   **National League Awards**

The Vikings had a very successful time at National League Awards Evening held at Elland Road, Leeds, with individual players, and the club, gaining recognition.

Dennis Moran's outstanding season for the Vikings saw him pick up the Player of the Year award for National League One, ahead of team-mate Ollie Wilkes. In addition to his inspirational performances in defence and attack Dennis found time to contribute 23 tries during 2007, several of which were trademark 'interception tries'. In addition the Vikings had six players named in the NL1 'Dream Team'. Moran and Bob Beswick were named for the second successive year, and were joined by team-mates Scott Grix, Damien Blanch, Mick Nanyn, and Ollie Wilkes in the following line-up:

Scott Grix, Damien Blanch, Michael Shenton (Castleford), Mick Nanyn, Danny Mills (Sheffield), Dennis Moran, Danny Brough (Castleford), Ollie Wilkes, Sean Penkywicz (Halifax), Mark Leafa (Castleford), Richard Fletcher (Whitehaven), Ryan Clayton (Castleford) and Bob Beswick.

A massive boost for the club came when Widnes were voted 'Club of the Year' for 2007. The judges based their decision on the work done by the Vikings both on and off the pitch in areas such as Community, Scholarship and the Service Area. In accepting the award on behalf of the Club, Chairman Peter Knowles said, "This is a tremendous achievement by everyone involved with Widnes Vikings. To win this award, in the face of stiff competition from other clubs, shows that the RFL recognises the work undertaken by the Club, and as we work towards the licensing process for 2009 this award gives us even more confidence that our bid for a licence for 2009-2011 will be successful.

4th October 2007   **Final Preparations**

After naming his squad Vikings boss Steve McCormack issued a rallying cry to fans ahead of the Grand Final, when he called for the town to roar his men back into Super League with a victory against Castleford in the Grand Final at Headingley.

He said: "Sometimes I don't think the fans realise just how important they are to the club. They have been a massive bonus to how we have done all year, but we need them now more than ever. We know exactly how important this is to the fans. They have stuck with us through thick and thin. But now we need them to make more noise than Cas because they can genuinely make a difference on the day."

Boosted by the return to fitness of Aaron Summers, McCormack was confident that his men could go one step further than last year. "We know what we have to do and know we can do it," he said. "As I've said all season, when we play at our best we can beat anyone in this division and that still stands. We have been a bit lacklustre in the closing games of the season, but we showed against Halifax that there is still a great deal of passion in the squad. And the most important part was that we won it. We played as well as we have done all season for large parts of the game and we just have to produce that kind of football against Castleford," adding "There will be a lot of nerves when this weekend comes around, but we have to look at this match as a must-win and forget the occasion, but we have the players who have the experience to be able to do that. Everyone is really excited about it and we all just want to get on with the job." McCormack went on to pick out Mark Smith, Scott Grix and Damien Blanch for their inspirational performances in the 36-24 play-off semi-final win over Halifax. "They were incredible on Sunday and will be expecting more of the same this weekend," he said. "There was a level of intensity that we have been aiming for all year. We went to Castleford and beat them. We know we can do it and I am sure they will not be expecting an easy game. It will be a class match and I am sure it will be value for money for everyone watching it. If we can't produce it against Castleford in a game like the Grand Final, we don't deserve promotion to Super League. It's that simple."

7th October 2007 - NL1 Grand Final
Headingley Carnegie Stadium, Leeds

Castleford Tigers   42
Widnes Vikings   10

If the emotions leaving Warrington 12 months ago were of abject despair, this time round they were indescribable - a rare concoction of disappointment, misery, tears, and yes anger! Although out-numbered on the day the Vikings fans heading to Leeds, in a black and white convoy of coaches and cars, were quietly confident of winning 'the one that really mattered'. For my part, thinking back to last year I had emptied my head of any omens that attempted to take up residence. But was that in itself an omen?

The crowd built steadily as we watched former Vikings

Andy Kain, Adam Hughes, Lucas Onyango and James Coyle take part in the NL2 Final, with Kain's Featherstone Rovers overcoming the Oldham Roughyeds.

Finally the moment arrived that we had all been anticipating - for 365 days - as the players came out to do battle, with Paul Noone animatedly encouraging the fans to get behind the team. However the anticipation dissipated within the first 60 seconds as Castleford were awarded a penalty for a high tackle by Mick Cassidy, which Brough casually knocked over from 35 metres. With Castleford appearing to show more urgency in their play Widnes hearts were in their mouths again in the fifth minute when the Tigers appeared to cross for a try. The 'score' was ruled out by Ian Smith, the video referee, but he awarded them a penalty - again converted by Brough. Mr Smith came to the rescue again some five minutes later when he again ruled out a Castleford try.

Gradually the Vikings gained more possession and better position, but they were knocked back following a rare handling error by Dennis Moran only 10 metres from his line. Collecting a grubber kick from Brough the stand off coughed up possession as he was tackled and the ball was immediately fed to Wainwright who cut inside to score. Although Brough missed the conversion he added a 'one pointer' minutes later to give his side a 9 - 0 advantage. The Vikings then put together their first concerted attack on the Castleford line before a booming '40/20' by Brough set them back on the attack, with McGoldrick on the end of the move to cross for another unconverted try.

Widnes looked dangerous on the rare occasions that they found themselves near the Castleford line, and they finally capitalised on this in the 35th minute when Mick Nanyn scored his 28th try of the season. Having moved deep into 'Cas territory Toa Kohe-Love, Damien Blanch and Mark Smith all threatened the line before Smith switched play to the left with

Bob Beswick firing a short pass to Nanyn who, taking four defenders with him, scored from eight yards out. With Noone again acting as motivator-in-chief and buoyed by this success the Vikings came close to further reducing the arrears as half-time approached. The ball was moved smartly along the 40 metre line into the hands of Nanyn, who broke two tackles before off-loading to Noone just inside the Castleford half, who in turn passed inside to Scott Grix on the '30'. Gaining a few extra yards the fullback slipped a pass to Joel Penny who was racing up in support only for the scrum-half to fail to gather the ball, with Moran by his side and the line at their mercy. With a deficit of only three points the Vikings would have gone in at half-time with a renewed confidence, but it remained 13 - 4 at the break.

Needing to register the first score of the second period the Vikings had their supporters on their feet within seconds as Nanyn again crossed the line - but this time the attention of four defenders 'held him up' to prevent the score. From the re-start Widnes forced a repeat set and from this Grix was inches from scoring a spectacular individual try. Having carried the ball back to the Castleford '20' the Vikings passed the ball around before finally Moran fed Beswick who in turn brought Grix into the action. The fullback, faced with no support, kicked 'in goal' from 15 metres before having to take the circular route around a defender only to be foiled by a last ditch soccer-style sliding tackle from Dixon.

Within two minutes Widnes' renewed urgency and enthusiasm had all but evaporated when in the next attack Brough completely wrong-footed the defence to collect his own chip, before putting Guttenbeil over under the sticks before adding the easy conversion. The stubborn and resilient defence, which had been the platform for Widnes' dominance for much of the season, could no longer withstand the relentless pressure from

Castleford and conceded a further try to a fine passing movement finished off by Shenton in the 52nd minute.

As Widnes ran out of creative ideas a second drop goal from Brough was the prelude to two further scores, as first Westerman dived over from dummy half and then Clayton scored by the corner flag to give Castleford a 36 - 4 lead with fifteen minutes remaining. In July Widnes fans had heckled the Whitehaven fans who left Bloomfield Road early, but at this point felt it was their turn to make an early start to their journey home.

Those that had left missed the final, defiant act by two of the most consistent players of the season as Nanyn converted a try from the whole-hearted Oliver Wilkes in the 69th minute. Smith had intercepted a Brough chip inside his own half and advanced into the opposition half before waiting for support to arrive. Ian Webster was eventually halted eight metres out, and from the play-the-ball Wilkes ran on to a pass from Smith to charge over in typical fashion from 10 metres.

With just five minutes left Guttenbeil added his second try to enable Brough to take the final score to a demoralising 42 - 10, and but for an outstanding defensive display from Scott Grix, who covered and tackled across the width of the pitch, the margin of defeat could have been even worse.

Dignified as ever Steve McCormack faced up to his fourth successive Grand Final defeat by admitting that "We saved our worst performance for the most important game of the season. It's hard for anybody associated with Widnes to take. Castleford were far superior from the first second to the last."

Tigers: Donlan, Williams, McGoldrick, Shenton, Dixon, Thackeray, Brough, Higgins, Henderson, Guttenbeil, Clayton, Charles, Westerman. Subs: Wainwright, Leafa, Lupton, Boyle

Tries: Wainwright, McGoldrick, Shenton, Guttenbeil (2), Westerman, Clayton

Goals: Brough (7)

Vikings: Grix, Blanch, Kohe-Love, Nanyn, Dodd, Moran, Penny, Cassidy, Smith, Wilkes, Tomkins, Noone, Beswick. Subs: Summers, James, Webster, Doran

Tries: Nanyn, Wilkes

Goal: Nanyn

Referee: Phil Bentham   Att: 20,814

CHAPTER SEVEN

Final Whistle

PHEEEEEP!!

As Phil Bentham blew the final whistle of the 2007 season the hopes and expectations of all concerned with Widnes Vikings - management, coaching staff, players and fans alike - were finally extinguished. That whistle set in motion a dramatic chain of events which saw the club pass through an emotional, painful, but ultimately successful metamorphosis which culminated in an optimistic future under new ownership.

After the surprising but welcome return of Steve McCormack, Paul Cook and the Head Coach looked back on the final weeks of the season and forward to 2008. Paul's interview is reproduced here:

The season ended in bitter disappointment both on and off the field, after Widnes fans had harboured such high hopes in mid-season.

Castleford ran away with the Grand Final to secure their Super League place, and the Vikings were plunged into administration, prompting an exodus of players and a genuine sense of uncertainty about the club's future.

After several weeks with no solution in sight, coach Steve McCormack was one of those who reluctantly moved on, joining Hull KR as assistant to head coach Justin Morgan.

But the season's drama was not yet over.

Local businessman Steve O'Connor stepped in to take the club over, a new board structure was put in place, a high-profile sponsor secured, and McCormack persuaded to return and help rebuild the side.

Back at the newly named Stobart Stadium Halton, he described how defeat in the Grand Final had triggered a remarkable chain of events.

With the Northern Rail Cup final in Blackpool, Widnes appeared to have peaked too soon, never hitting the heights of that performance again. But McCormack believes the performance against Whitehaven was one of those days when everything comes together and wasn't, perhaps, indicative of how the side could play week in and week out.

Also, when other sides are scrapping harder for points at the business end of the season, it sometimes needs the ability to just get the job done

"I think we, the coaches and the players, set ourselves such high standards in the early part of the season, the spectators perhaps expected a Blackpool-style performance every week and that was never going to happen.

"Even though we weren't playing to that kind of level afterwards I thought some of our performances showed we really had to grind out and win in different ways, although I think it's fair to say that we didn't reach the levels of the early part of the season.

"I wouldn't say the Northern Rail Cup was perfect but what I would say was that it was as good as I've seen a team execute for a long time.

"We did play well in some of the back end of the year games but when people compared it to that final it was perceived that we were stuttering along a bit.

"But those games still had to be won and the teams we were playing still had something to play for whether it was a top two place, top six or avoiding relegation.

"There was a lot at stake at the back end of the season and you sometimes have to grind results out which we did up to the final."

Compared to the previous season, which had seen Grand Final preparations disrupted by knocks to several players, Widnes had a relatively straightforward build-up this time around.

"We didn't have any problems to be fair going into the final. I had to leave a couple of players out, but we didn't have any excuses."

What Widnes faced at Headingley was a Castleford team that turned in a devastating performance from the word go.

Widnes passed up a couple of opportunities in the closing minutes of the first half and at the start of the second which, if taken, might have put some doubts in the minds of the Tigers, but otherwise they were worthy winners – a fact McCormack was quick to acknowledge.

"They started well and one thing we identified early on in the week was that we had to get at Danny Brough and make sure that he wasn't playing in a dinner suit as was quoted on the television. But he did, and like Danny Brough is capable of doing he took the game by the scruff of the neck.

"I thought Castleford were excellent and to be honest we were dominated and never really in the game. In finals you've got to take your chances. Castleford were clinical in everything that they did. We had a couple of chances but only took one out of three.

"Castleford played like we did in the Northern Rail Cup and took every opportunity. We weren't as good with the last pass as we should have been. Either side of half-time we had chances where we could have ended up being in front and if we'd taken either one it could have been a different story, but that's sport isn't it?

"But I've no complaints we were beaten by a far better side on the day. We'd played them four times previously and there had been nothing between us."

What happened next shocked Widnes supporters as the club announced it was going into administration, but McCormack was already aware of the likely damage caused by failing to get into Super League.

"The fall out wasn't a surprise to me. I knew going into the game what was at stake and what the circumstances would be if we didn't win it, which is obviously what happened.

"A lot of people turned up for work on the Monday morning and were in shock. When you're told you might possibly lose your jobs, that comes down to more than whether you enjoy the game every week – it's about people's livelihoods, mortgages and families and anyone who has been in that situation knows it's not a nice place to be.

"Certain players had probably agreed deals before the game with other teams in case we didn't win. But that's not an excuse or to say that their heads weren't on the game.

"It's to do with the timing of the Grand Final. From September time you can start talking to players and because of the situation the club probably couldn't offer a lot of deals out."

It quickly became apparent that whatever shape the club was in, the team would need to be completely rebuilt as the player drain began in earnest.

"A lot of players went straight away and a lot went in the first week. From my point of view I turned a National League 1 team down in the first week, a National League 2 team down in the second week and it was three weeks before I decided to go to Hull KR and that was purely because there are not many head coach jobs available.

"I was with Scotland in Glasgow in preparation for the Wales game. I'd agreed to go to Hull KR and was looking forward to working with Justin Morgan, with the squad that they had and working in Super League, and it was a big wrench to be leaving here."

But the upheaval wasn't quite over. Widnes were brought out of administration and the new team in charge wanted a familiar face to oversee the rebuilding process.

"I hadn't started at Hull KR and on a Thursday night I got a phone call asking if I would be interested in meeting Steve O'Connor which was a big surprise.

"I nipped back to see my family and I met Steve at the

Haydock Thistle and within five minutes of what he was telling me about the club and his ambitions for it, I agreed to return. What he said was something that the club has needed for a long, long time."

Extricating himself from his new position at Hull KR could have been a messy proposition, but McCormack has nothing but praise for the way the business was conducted.

"It was right that we did things properly and the way it was handled with Hull KR was as good as I've ever known it. From their point of view it was a nightmare and I realised I was letting them down. But I spoke with Justin Morgan and told him my reasons, and the way he, their Chairman and Chief Executive dealt with it was absolutely superb."

Stepping back into the Widnes coaching position, McCormack was under no illusions about the size of the role.

"It was a big task and I knew the challenge when I spoke with Steve O'Connor, and it's probably the biggest I've ever had. It was a big decision for Steve to bring me back and it was nice that he was showing a bit of confidence in me.

"Bearing in mind clubs are starting to sign players in September it shows just what a massive task it was to start putting a team together.

"Credit to the lads who stayed - the famous five as they've become known. I was in daily contact with them and a few of the younger players. Some of the younger ones left when I went to Hull KR because they didn't know exactly what was happening and I'm still in contact with them now.

"But to get players with experience like Jim Gannon and Iain Morrison helped and from having no club we've got a squad capable of competing in National League 1.

"It was a big challenge but one I couldn't turn down. I've never been one to turn a challenge down."

He said that the changes at the club had definitely had a

positive effect on the playing side of the organisation.

"That's no disrespect to the previous boards I worked under. I worked under Tony Chambers and Tom Fleet and they were really good to me, Stephen Vaughan really backed us when he first came in and enabled me to bring in Damien Blanch, Dennis Moran, Ollie Wilkes and Jordan James so I had the support of them as well.

"But I think the whole organisation takes its lead from the top man and you look at what he has achieved in business and what he has brought in here in such a short time and it's absolutely phenomenal.

"The infrastructure away from the playing side is as good as anything; certainly the best in the National League.

"To give you an example of how things get done, I met an architect the day before I went on holiday on November 15th and he said ideally what would you want in the gym in the North Stand. So I told him, but thought that it might be a bit pie in the sky, and when I got back they'd already knocked walls down and it was in the process of being built, in consultation with myself, the physio and the conditioner.

"The club has never been like it is now, and with that comes extra pressure to succeed on the field and get the Super League licence with help from off the field."

That professional off-field approach was exemplified by a fans event to introduce the new men in charge, the new squad and launch the new kit. The stadium's biggest suite was absolutely packed.

"You only have to look at the launch to see the difference, the visual aids were fantastic. The players spent a full day at a studio for that five minute video to promote the kit and it was done absolutely to perfection.

"We realised then that this new guy certainly means business and the fans that turned up, well we could have filled it three times over, so it was fantastic from the fans' point of view."

That feeling of a new start will hopefully be equally apparent when visitors start arriving for the new season.

"What we want is that anyone who has previously been involved with the Vikings whenever they come to the club next season they walk through the door and realise it's not the same club. The club is genuinely the real deal.

"Prior to Steve O'Connor coming in people wrote the club off.

"We're nine points behind in the league already but it was the right decision for the Rugby League to take and we'll take it on the chin. The nine points is a big gap, and it'll be tough, but everyone has bought into what's going on here. The players are up for the challenge.

"And personally, I can't wait for the season."

Following the Grand Final defeat skipper Mark Smith gave the players perspective when he told Steven Kelly of the Runcorn & Widnes World that "We were all absolutely devastated after the game. We were a lot more disappointed about this defeat than last season's because we were really in with a massive shout. As it turned out we saved the poorest performance for the most important game and you just cannot do that. I think the scoreline flattered Cas, but I won't take anything away from them. We came up against a great Cas side - and in particular a very good Danny Brough."

But despite the loss, Smith praised the Widnes faithful who travelled to Leeds for the final. "The fans were great," he said. "I feel more disappointed for them than anyone. They were great on the day and cheered us off after such a bad display. There aren't many clubs that have that." On a personal note he added "They have been right behind me from day one. They have treated me superbly and they deserve better than this."

Speaking to the same newspaper, following his decision to follow Dennis Moran and Gareth Price to Leigh, Toa Kohe-Love spoke out about the effect, on the players and their careers, of the club going into Administration. "As soon as the Cas game finished rumours started flying around about the club being in trouble - it's a real shame because I enjoyed my time and it was the best bunch of guys I'd worked with." He claimed that the first the players knew of the seriousness of the situation was "when we were called in to sign some forms" and were told by the club "We're sorry, we're in trouble, there's nothing we can do." Underlining the spirit in the dressing room Kohe-Love added "On Mad Monday there were a couple of blokes crying, it was that much a shame to move on. But we were left with no choice - you can't hang on forever. With a fan base, a stadium and history like that they should be in Super League playing against Warrington, Wigan and Saints. It's a shame for the club to go the way it's gone."

Some weeks later, when I had the opportunity to speak to the 'famous five', it was plain to see, contrary to rumour and popular opinion, that there was a genuine love of the club, and respect for team-mates throughout the 2007 squad. Whilst these five (Mark Smith, Bob Beswick, Paul Noone, Gavin Dodd and Dean Gaskell) had for a variety of personal reasons felt able to turn down offers from other clubs - Super League in some cases - some of their colleagues, for equally valid reasons, had opted to secure their futures elsewhere.

Looking back on the season Smith said that "captaining the side to victory in the Northern Rail Cup Final" was the highlight of the season, but added that "I was equally as proud to lead the side to the Grand Final". Having left a Super League club to join Widnes it was a "massive disappointment, with such a fantastic squad", to again lose in the Grand Final. The skipper confirmed that with all the media and public interest confidence in the squad during the build up had been high: "In the four previous games we had battered them, and they had battered us, so we knew we had it in us. It was just a question of who turned up on the day, but we thought it would be a lot closer than it was".

Describing the post-match dressing room at Headingley as "not a nice place to be .... the quietest place you could have been" Mark highlighted the added frustration of a professional sportsman of "not having a game next week to put it right".

Bob Beswick, another to have sampled top level rugby league was, in common with his team-mates, keen to stay at Widnes, despite interest from three Super League Clubs. Admitting that "It was very tempting to sign for them", Beswick added "I really enjoyed the season at Widnes, despite the Grand Final, and I was always going to see what happened at the club. Widnes is a fantastic club with great supporters and with the right off field set up it could be as good if not better than most current Super League clubs". Like his colleagues Beswick came to Widnes "with a point to prove to Super League clubs", and although there is no automatic promotion in 2008 he is adamant that there will be plenty of motivation for the Widnes players in 2008. The Vikings vice-captain felt "the stature of the club, the professional desire to play every week, overcoming the 9 point penalty imposed by the RFL and the desire to achieve a Super League Licence" will provide all the incentive the players need. While the unity of the camp had been questioned in some quarters prior to the Grand Final Bob was firmly of the opinion that "you could tell from the effort that there was no split in the camp".

2007 saw Widnes born Paul Noone finally make his professional debut for his home-town club, having previously been rejected as a 13-year old. Explaining that "I was already training with Widnes when I was approached by Warrington, who eventually offered me a professional contract", Noone began a twelve year association with the local rivals, before Steve Mc-Cormack brought him 'home' for 2007. Another to receive overtures from other clubs he "loved last year" citing "wearing my first Widnes shirt along with appearing in my first finals as a professional player" as his personal highlights of the season. With a steadfast ambition of playing in Super League for the Vikings Paul added "I would have kicked myself if I had left and then found Widnes were in Super League for 2009".

For much of the season Dean Gaskell was playing 'catch up' having undergone a double hernia operation in the close season.. By mid-season he was getting into his stride when an injury to Damien Blanch gave him a run of first team opportunities in which to impress his coach. This bore fruit when "on the Thursday before the Northern Rail Cup Final Steve told me that I was in the team". Being in direct competition with Gavin Dodd for much of the season Gaskell added that the "competition in the squad, even in training" was intense and to the benefit of the team. Although having been on the 'wrong end' of some of his coach's selections during 2007, Dean was another who did not hesitate to sign for the Vikings "once Steve's (McCormack) return had been confirmed".

When Gavin Dodd was asked to name his personal highlight he also opted for the Grand Final, before almost reluctantly, adding his 'points in a match record'! Recognising the magnitude of his achievement, in eclipsing the previous record held jointly by Andy Currier and Jonathan Davies, Dodd said "when you were growing up these people were everybody's heroes, and Widnes were massive". Taking over the kicking duties from the absent Mick Nanyn at Doncaster, 'Doddy' was blissfully unaware of the record until he was handed the 'tee' with the words "you've just equalled the record - this one to beat it". A true 'club man' Gavin, who had completed his first full season as a full-time professional, admitted to favouring the fullback position, but was "happy to play in any position" for his coach, and was another to rubbish the rumours of a rift in the dressing room. Significantly, in view of those rumours, he confirmed that being in a "team environment on a daily basis created tremendous team spirit".

Unlike his four colleagues Dodd had been 'part-time' until the last month of the 2006 season and I was naturally interested to hear his views on the other benefits of full-time training. He told me "It has massive benefits. You can dedicate your time to getting into the best physical shape possible without having the problem of working 40 hours plus per week and then going training", as well as enabling "good diet and tactical advice on a daily basis".

Another key member of last season's footballing staff to sign a new contract was of course Head Coach Steve McCormack, who at a Fans Forum called by new owner Steve O'Connor, paid tribute to the 'famous five' for their loyalty to the cause, whilst conceding that he had actually 'left'!

McCormack had waited for three weeks, turning down two job offers in the process, before finally succumbing to the offer to join Hull KR. As he told me "good players will always get clubs, but coaches cannot afford to be out of the game, or they are easily forgotten". Whilst his thoughts on the season are covered in more detail through his interviews with Paul Cook, he confirmed the view that "nobody wanted to leave" and that some players had actually regretted leaving. He went on to say that during the team meeting on the Thursday before the Grand Final "every player stood up in turn and they all said they wanted to stay" in the event that Widnes gained promotion, and that the concensus amongst the players was that this was "the best group of players they had each worked with".

If proof were needed of the spirit within the camp the

Head Coach cited Gavin Dodd's reaction to missing out on selection for the Northern Rail Cup Final. "It was the hardest decision I've had to make" but Doddy reacted by "coming into the dressing room to wish everybody good luck before taking his seat for the match".

McCormack was honest enough to admit though that there was one sour note as a small, mindless minority vented their inability to accept defeat at Headingley with a personal attack on the Head Coach. As mentioned elsewhere in this book he had weathered the storm of irrational abuse in the early days of his Widnes career. There was unfortunately a case of déjà vu when, in the wake of this admittedly poor performance, there were some who saw fit to allege that the 'club meant nothing to Steve McCormack' because they felt that he had 'snubbed' the crowd on the final whistle at Headingley.

The truth of the matter is that, having suffered the bitter taste of defeat at the final hurdle for the fourth year in a row, he completed his interview commitments, before going to his family. He then went into the dressing room where, having ejected the 'Rugby League Raw' cameras, he composed himself and recognising the implications of defeat, talked to his players and coaching staff in private.

I would venture to suggest that Steve McCormack did nothing to disrespect the club or its fans during his tenure at the then Halton Stadium. Hurt as he must undoubtedly have been by this outburst, he surely demonstrated his affection for Widnes Vikings by immediately recinding his decision to join Hull KR when Steve O'Connor asked him to return to Widnes. He was rightly given rapturous applause when 're-introduced' to the faithful at the Fans Forum.

However, whilst the coach and players were collectively responsible for events on the pitch, they had no input into the decisions and actions taking place behind the scenes that would have a massive effect on their careers and livelihoods, as the club entered Administration.

While Dean Gaskell confirmed that the players were unaware of the financial implications of defeat he admitted that it was a shock "to go from the euphoria of playing in a Grand Final, in front of a full house, to find that 24 hours later you had no job". Mark Smith had found it "surreal for a club like Widnes to be in this position, and after nine years as a professional I even considered going part-time and returning to college or even packing in". Demonstrating the commitment of the players to the Widnes cause the skipper added that "what was really good was the way the lads all stuck together during the following month". All the players, from junior to senior professionals were ringing each other, and the club, daily as they hung on in the hope of a quick resolution to the ownership issue.

Whilst it is always of interest to hear the thoughts and opinions of our sporting heroes, it must be remembered that in addition to its playing and coaching staff the other vital ingredient of any sporting organisation is its fans, who turn up in all weathers to support 'their club'. Unlike the players and other employees of Widnes Vikings the fans' ability to pay their bills and support their families had not been put in jeopardy. Nonetheless the emotional pain suffered by those fans should not be underestimated, and it is only right then that, in a book like this, they were given the opportunity to have their thoughts, highs and lows, recorded. A selection is included below:

Before returning from Blackpool, Widnes Vikings played some of the most enterprising attractive rugby that the lower leagues have probably ever seen. More offloads than ever before with even our wingers scoring tries on the overlap. We thrashed Castleford at Cas by offloading them to death!

On returning from Blackpool, our tactics changed thereon to the 'Phil Larder Method' of down the middle. Why? Who knows? If only we had continued to play attractive rugby all season, maybe we would have managed to beat Castle'Brough'ford in Leeds.

We are a winning team when playing attractive rugby.

Carl Hill

Where do I begin? What a season it was, full of elation and ultimately disappointment. The feeling of invincibility after Nanyn's try against Whitehaven in the final few minutes of a game that seemed to be slipping away. This feeling was cruelly taken away by one man. Danny Brough! A name that will forever bring a shudder to the spine of every Widnes supporter. It was interesting to see the slow turning of the pendulum as Castleford turned the momentum their way with a thrilling 18-24 win at Widnes in August, sadly giving us little time to swing it back.

Colin Vickerstaff

On the field overall the lads performed throughout the whole of the season. The highlight was on the 17th May 2007 at Wheldon Road, Castleford in the league in front of the Sky Television cameras. Both sides tested one another from the start and this was to prove to be our greatest win of last year. Blackpool was also special, the emphatic win, the lifting of the Northern Rail Cup but nothing compared to that famous cold night in Castleford. Its hard to believe how one minute everything was so perfect both on and off the field and then to see the World famous club go into Administration, its a crying shame.

Ian Waterworth.

It was the first time me, my husband Carl and 2 sons, Ian & Sean had been to a cup final. What a day! The atmosphere, people who you didn't know talking to you and all these in-flated balls being thrown around the crowd. Fantastic! When Mark Smith lifted that cup, us and everyone went mad, we had lost most of our voices due to shouting and cheering the lads on. And I still get goosebumps thinking about it. It was a fantastic day out and one I'll never forget.

Jackie Peck

I took my son, Liam, aged 5, to see the Vikings for his first time against Wigan in the Challenge Cup. He was so excited, with the crowd and atmosphere and had his picture taken stood next to the trophy. He made me laugh when he said "dad, why are there girls playing?" he was referring to Mick Cassidy and Damien Blanch - he got confused with their long hair. After a fantastic season, all our hopes were dashed at the final in Leeds, but we stayed to the end to cheer the players on their good season. Liam wasn't too disappointed, he was made up because he had got a Vikings flag to wave about. His favourite player is Mick Nanyn. We are both looking forward to 2008 season, lets get back where we belong.

Colin and Liam Clarke

Being a Widnesian exile living in Glasgow, I don't get to see as many games as I would like. However, on the day of the Northern Rail cup final I was on holiday in Cala Llonga on Ibiza and looking forward to the game. Ten minutes before kick off, I asked the barmaid at my hotel - in my best Spanish - to puede poner el Sky Sports tres so that I could watch the game. She found the channel, when the only other person in the bar, a large Scotsman, requested that it be put back to the Scottish Open. I beat a hasty retreat in a quest to find another bar. I managed to find one and sat with 2 Yorkshire lads who joined me in watching Widnes v Whitehaven. They were not big Rugby League fans, but thoroughly enjoyed the match, commenting that Widnes were like the Harlem Globetrotters and scoring for fun. I was proud of my team that day.

Davie Roberts

I have been a member of The Supporters Club since June 1957. At that time we sold 'penny on the ball', helped with the tea bars and the licensed bars to raise money for the club and in 1962 I started to run the coaches to away games. I was elected chairman in 1973. During my time as chairman the good times have far outweighed the bad, winning every piece of silverware available (apart from The Yorkshire Cup) During the 90`s the club experienced some hard times as they tried to keep up with the changing face of Rugby League. However Season 2007 will be forever etched in my memory because of the rollercoaster ride the club took the supporters on. The superb quality of Rugby League we witnessed for long spells , the high point at Blackpool, the depths of despair at Headingley and the high point when our new owners secured the clubs future. The future is bright, the future is Widnes Vikings.

Alan Rae
Chairman, Widnes Vikings Supporters Club

Season 2007 will go down in history as a turning point in the history of Widnes Rugby League Club. During the season the range of emotions that fans went through was incredible. The excitement as our team took to the field and played fast free flowing rugby (something we had not seen for years), the pride the passion and the jubilation we experienced at Blackpool, the humiliation at Headingley, the desperation as administration was announced and finally the delight, expectation and anticipation that Mr O`Connor's purchase of the club has brought.

Onwards and upwards. You can't keep a good club down for ever.

Noreen Curphey

I come up on a regular basis to see my family that live up here and to watch Widnes play whenever they are playing, home or away. The best away journey had to be when I went to Wales to watch Widnes against the Celtic Crusaders. It took us 9 hours to get down there and the weather was absolutely awful. We got there in the end, but, it was the wrong stadium, we ended up at a coal mine. Well, maybe it was the right stadium but they didn't want to embarrass themselves so they sent us to a different stadium. We got to the game, Widnes won. We then got back on the coach all the way back to Widnes but it only took us about 5 hours. The closest game to where I live was in London. That was the game where Widnes thrashed London Scholars. That took me about an hour to get to and the people who live in Widnes took about 5 hours to get there. Overall this season I was very pleased with the games that I went to as they won about 99% of them. I hope Widnes do as well as they did this season and wish all the new players and owner the best of luck.

Jack from Watford

CHAPTER EIGHT

Press Conference

The Co-Operative's sponsorship deal with the National Leagues was unveiled at Headingley back in March and I remember that, at the event, all the talk was about the battle between the big two, Castleford and Widnes, for promotion. No other team really got a mention although it was agreed that you couldn't rule Whitehaven out.

And when Widnes started their National League campaign live on Sky with a 46-12 demolition of Leigh Centurions that seemed to confirm the view that Steve McCormack's experienced and tough side would take some stopping. Dennis Moran was on fire that night, getting his first hat trick of the season and they looked a classy outfit. And that win had been preceded by a great performance in defeat against Wigan in the Challenge Cup.

But the rugby league rumour mill was buzzing with stories of behind the scenes problems at Widnes so it wasn't a massive surprise when chairman Stephen Vaughan resigned. The doom mongers reckoned that was the end of their season,that the team would fall apart, but the players had the perfect response.

The 44-20 win at Castleford strengthened the Vikings case and showed they weren't going to let the off pitch dramas affect them. Steve McCormack, who's been through a lot already as a coach, remained optimistic and humorous although I think my Rab C Nesbitt reference – in honour of his Scottish coaching role – was below the belt.

Talking of below the belt, Vikings conditioner Andy Haigh lifted the lid on the coaching staff's dietary habits – cheesy chips was one of their post-training session favourites.

The Vikings 100 per cent record was ended on a miserable night at the Shay by Halifax. The writing wasn't exactly on the wall but it did show that Widnes were vulnerable against committed and physical opponents.

They won the Northern Rail Cup with ease against White-haven but that has always been a poisoned chalice – the last three teams to win that have then failed to earn promotion.

And so it proved. Castleford, second best to the Vikings in the first half of the season, turned the tables with two crucial wins, taking top spot in the table and then winning the qualifying play off. Widnes saw off a determined Halifax effort to qualify for the Grand Final but it can't be easy to prepare a side for such a crucial game when your key players are being linked with moves to rival clubs.

The Viking army descended on Headingley but a season that had begun with such justifiably high hopes for the fans ended with bitter disappointment. Castleford looked like a club heading for Super League. Widnes, as it turned out just a few days later, were heading for administration.

Bill Arthur
Sky Sports

Having spent a very enjoyable year as a player at Widnes in 2006 where we lost in the play off final I was looking forward to commenting on lots of National League fixtures including plenty of matches that involved Widnes. The 2007 season was one of "shit or bust" for Widnes. Everything was positive in the beginning with some fantastic early season form including an exciting display against Wigan which, in all fairness, Widnes was very unlucky to lose 24-34 in the Carnegie Challenge Cup. That game was watched by a bumper crowd and was an early sign of what was in store for the first three quarters of the season. With a narrow 18-12 victory over Castleford in the Northern Rail Semi Final, Widnes looked like there was no team in that division that would come anywhere near them, victory in the Final gave them an "invincible" tag.

Apart from a minor hic up against Halifax it seemed justified until Castleford in August beat the Vikings and then defeated them another two times including the Final.

On the coaching front I've worked with Steve McCormack and Andy Haigh and consider them to be hard working, knowledgeable, very thorough and bloody nice lads as well. The quality of players was better than most other teams in NL1 and there was no lack of commitment from them. The board put time and effort into recruitment and keeping those players happy so their level of commitment was very high as well. As history tells us the drama of 2007 was to come directly after the play off final when it emerged that every single egg that anybody owned in Widnes was put in one giant basket..! I can't say I portion any blame to anybody really if the game was won nobody would have known and Widnes Vikings would have been in Super League. In November Steve McCormack agreed to come back to the Club having provisionally agreeing to leave (which I know he didn't ever want to leave, despite what fans think none of the people in Rugby League are Millionaires and still need to pay bills) and I know he won't rest until he has done the job he set out to do originally… GET WIDNES BACK IN THE TOP BRACKET….!

Widnes is a name associated with Rugby League around the world. I have been fortunate during my career to play at the highest level against some the biggest names in the game and I can say without a shadow of a doubt that the Widnes club is one of the few teams in world rugby that everyone knows about. I personally hope that they are back at the top as soon as possible and the current blip is something that only serves to make the club stronger in the future.

Barrie McDermott

Inevitably, Widnes Vikings 2007 campaign will be judged by many purely in the light of their final game. The 42-10 mauling at the hands of Castleford Tigers in the Co-Operative National League One grand final at Headingley was a hammer blow to the club and its fans. The Vikings main goal for the year had been to gain promotion to Super League. Unfortunately, only one place was up for grabs and Castleford, deservedly, took it.

The margin of defeat hurt the fans badly. Messageboards and phone-ins were swamped by Widnes speccies with an array of theories about what had gone wrong in the final.

Passion, as it so often does, merely served to cloud judgement. But at the end of the day, it was a case of Castleford being very good and Widnes not being good enough.

Attempts at a fuller analysis inevitably lead to speculation because the truth of the matter is, nobody knows all the answers. Suggestions that players 'weren't trying' or should 'hang their heads in shame' are unedifying, unhelpful and unfair. What actually happened was one of those things sport occasionally throws at you.

Hitherto all-conquering St Helens suffered the same fate a week later in the Super League grand final having gone into the match as favourites. Few of the press box neutrals I spoke to after Headingley were over-surprised by the outcome.

The off-field fallout from Widnes's defeat was worse than most people could have envisaged with the club in the grip of a financial crisis and entering administration. But now, they're on the way back with a new regime at the helm.

And a more considered look back at 2007 tells you the Vikings played some excellent rugby league. A 44-20 away win over Castleford in May and the 54-6 annihilation of Whitehaven in Northern Rail Cup final at Blackpool two months later obviously stand out.

Hopefully, more days in the sun await the Widnes club in the near future.

John Lawless
Liverpool Echo

The 2007 season was one of the most turbulent at the club in recent times. Widnes fans experienced the incredible high of winning their first piece of silverware since the club won promotion in 2001 and the devastating low of losing another Grand Final at a time when the stakes couldn't be higher with the drawbridge for Super League about to be raised another notch.

Widnes Vikings' season began on a low note and effectively ended on one when the club lost out to Castleford Tigers for a place in Super League and was plunged into voluntary administration.

In regards to the Cooperative National League One campaign, things couldn't have started any worse for the Vikings, as the then chairman, Stephen Vaughan, had quit on the opening night of the season – the day the Vikings had to negotiate a tricky clash with Leigh Centurions. The Vikings went on to humiliate Leigh in front of the Sky Sports cameras with a 46-12 thrashing and that set an early benchmark for the season.

Widnes went on to land five consecutive victories before clashing with promotion favourites Castleford at the Jungle. The Widnes performance that night was nearly faultless as they easily dispatched Terry Matterson's men.

One of the highs of the season would be in the Challenge Cup, the famous trophy the Vikings had lofted no fewer than seven times. Widnes took on old rivals Wigan and many were expecting the Warriors and their new Aussie signing Trent Barrett to rip the Vikings to shreds. But McCormack's men showed real heart, guts and passion and put in a performance that would have beaten many teams in the lower reaches of the top flight.

Another highlight would be the Vikings' crushing victory over Whitehaven in the final of the Northern Rail Cup in Blackpool. Widnes played their best football of the season that day and they destroyed a very capable 'Haven side. From that point Widnes's season began to turn. The performance at Blackpool could not be reproduced.

The Vikings had previously matched Castleford in desire, talent and ruthlessness but the huge difference was that the Tigers had hit form at the right time. Widnes were still winning but they couldn't hit top gear in the run up to biggest game of the season.

Widnes fans and everyone connected with the club were having to come to terms with the fact that another season in the National League beckoned. This is no disgrace, however.

The Vikings as a club and a whole package, in my opinion, were not ready for the top flight. How could a side so close to the edge survive in Super League? The financial problems of the club were well documented and although Steven Vaughan had predicted the eventual administration the day the season began, the Vikings couldn't pull enough finance together for to stay afloat.

McCormack and Vaughan had put together the strongest side possible to challenge for the Grand Final by spending every penny of the salary cap and budget. They came one performance short and that is no embarrassment. If the Vikings had won that day, the off-field financial troubles would have still remained. But the reality of the situation is that the Vikings' future is now brighter than it has been for some time under a new owner.

The club had needed an overhaul for over a decade and that

would never have happened if the club had won on October 7, 2007.

But now I feel the club has a chance of restructuring and rebuilding with the new owner Steve O'Connor and head coach, Steve McCormack, working in harmony.

Ian Cheveau
Liverpool Daily Post

Just like all Widnes supporters I was very disappointed to see the Club fail at the last hurdle to get back into Super League and dismayed to see the Club go straight into administration. The Club is very important to the town and to the Borough of Halton, I know from travels around the UK and abroad that most people know of Widnes because of its Rugby League team.

During the season the highlight for me was the fantastic performance in the Northern Rail Cup Final at Blackpool where the team just demolished Whitehaven with a powerful performance and brilliant quick flowing Rugby League football. I also thought the support for the team was magnificent that afternoon from the start to the finish of the game. The noise generated by our supporters was superb. I did however go away from that match with a slight nagging doubt about whether we could match that performance in the play-off final, which I had no doubt the team would get to.

I am proud to be one of the club sponsors and give what ever support to the Club I can. This is sometimes by way of supporting the club in making representations to the Government over visa applications for overseas players, which I have done on a number of occasions successfully.

One of the priorities for the future, apart from putting together a winning team, must be how the club can generate more interest from the local community and get more people in to watch the side. For the future success of the Club it is vital more and more seats are filled in the Stadium and that may mean being much more innovative in the pricing structure. It is also very important we get more local players in the team, which I believe will help bring in more local support.

Widnes Vikings are a famous Club and have massive potential, with the right backing and leadership I believe we can be back up there with the best again

Derek Twigg MP

I find the current plight of Widnes very sad indeed. There but for the grace of god go several clubs! It's a disappointing, but true, trend that modern professional sport is more about managing finances, with clubs dependent on banks or benefactors. I only saw two matches last season, with contrasting performances - against Wigan in the Challenge Cup they played exceptionally well but were comprehensively beaten by Castleford in the Grand Final. With new owners and a better understanding of what's happened in the past they must rebuild for a franchise. The town, and the fans who have been very supportive and knowledgeable, need it. But it mustn't be taken for granted because every other club will claim to have the same right to be in Super League.

Jonathan Davies

When I look at my personal situation I have mixed feelings about my short time as a Director and then Chairman of the club. On one hand the club was trading at a loss from day one and in financial terms the 22 months I spent on the board, the last 5 as Chairman, cost me more than I could really afford to lose. On the other hand I put a lot of hours into the club, which was something I was quite happy to do. I met and worked with some really good people. I got involved with many areas at the club including the Academy, the Scholarship and the Service Area, and enjoyed every minute of that. I was the clubs representative at the RFL and represented the club at various supporter group meetings.

Being no longer involved with the club has left a big hole in my life but I assure you I will always be a Vikings supporter.

The aim of the club is of course to be in Super League, where I think we should be, but it is not going to be easy. Clearly Celtic Crusaders would appear to be certainties for a franchise and Salford will also be making a very strong bid.

Going into administration should turn out to be the best for the long term future of the club. Other clubs such as Hull KR have come out of administration much stronger. The new owner Steve O'Connor has been able to acquire the club completely debt free and he now has a better chance of taking the club forward successfully. I wish Steve all the very best for the future. It's a new era and let's hope it's a successful one.

Peter Knowles
Former Chairman, Widnes Vikings

There was hardly a single person in the Headingley press conference that didn't feel a heap of sympathy for Steve McCormack in the aftermath of Widnes Vikings' NL1 Grand Final defeat. A popular figure among the media, it was not difficult to see the pain of a fourth straight Grand Final defeat, and the dignified manner in which he responded to questions - something a few top flight coaches would do well to replicate - simply strengthened those feelings.

McCormack, of course, would probably rather the press felt anything but sympathy for him - but still, the way in which he conducted himself at what must have been an awful few minutes was a great credit. The side that he assembled had, in his own words, put in one of their worst performances of the year in by far their most important match.

How he must have wished that they reproduced the form of their stunning away win at Castleford in the league, or the way in which they clinically dismantled Whitehaven in the Northern Rail Cup final. Unfortunately for the Vikings and McCormack, those matches will not form the lasting memories of 2007.

Even the Grand Final heartache may be overtaken in those terms in years to come by the events of the days after the Tigers defeat, when the very future of Widnes Vikings Rugby League Club was placed in doubt. But after a hairy few weeks, the club survived, and quickly re-instated McCormack as coach. Both he and everyone involved with the Vikings will be hoping there are no feelings of sympathy come the end of the 2008 campaign.

Gareth Walker
League Weekly

What a year to be a Widnes Vikings fan?

A cup success, a nail-biting tussle for the National League One championship, club records smashed and one game which almost brought about the end of the historic side – not quite your bog standard rugby league campaign.

Steve McCormack's men were quite rightly - along with rivals Castleford - tipped for promotion to Super League as they ran riot with a string of outstanding performances. Throughout the early stages of the season, there was a sense that - after losing out to Hull KR in the Grand Final in the previous campaign - McCormack's side would go one better this time around.

There was a buzz around Widnes. Even the mighty Wigan found it tough as they struggled to a narrow 34-24 victory over Widnes in the Challenge Cup. And a stunning victory over Castleford in their own back yard only added to the hype that the club was heading back to Super League. However, it all changed in June when an ill-fated trip to Halifax saw the Vikings lose their 100 per cent league record - and their nerve.

Knocking Castleford out of the Northern Rail Cup the following match and eventually lifting the trophy three weeks later with a stunning win over Whitehaven in Blackpool went some way to lifting the spirits at Halton Stadium, but the defeat at the Shay exposed weaknesses in Widnes' once-impenetrable back line. The side continued to play some excellent rugby throughout the season under new skipper Mark Smith - most notably Mick Nanyn, who celebrated a double whammy by breaking the points and goals records for a season. But while the team's performances were impressively turning heads, it was a different story behind the scenes.

Former owner Stephen Vaughan put the club up for sale and stood down, which many believed was a worrying sign of things to come. And so it proved. Two successive defeats to Castleford meant Widnes had to settle for second best in League One and ended all hopes of a return to the top flight. More alarmingly, however, was the club's demise into administration following Vikings' appalling loss to Cas in the Grand Final.

The announcement shook the sport. A once all-conquering outfit threatened with going out of business. Who would have though it 20 years ago? The squad has been all but decimated by the news as a mass exodus of players left Widnes with little hope of survival. But it was millionaire businessman Steve O'Connor - together with Halton Borough Council - who saved the club from the chop with an ambitious rescue package.

Vikings begin the forthcoming season with a nine-point deduction for going into administration, but all efforts are on securing a Super League franchise in 2009. Only time will tell if O'Connor, McCormack and co. can pull it off.

Steven Kelly
Runcorn & Widnes World

How will we remember 2007?

More than likely, as a season that almost saw the club go under, only for it to re-emerge in possibly a stronger position structurally that it had been in for years.

On the field, the excitement of lifting the Northern Rail Cup was somewhat nullified by the pain of a second successive Grand Final defeat. The performances against Whitehaven in the NRC final at Blackpool and the comprehensive league win against Castleford on their own ground were high spots of the first half of the season that unfortunately couldn't be repeated in the second.

Off the field, the descent into administration was the darkest of days, but the takeover by a new administration held great promise for the future.

I'm looking forward to seeing that promise fulfilled.

Paul Cook

'Do you realise that this is the most important match in our history', that was the bold statement as we travelled hopefully to Headingley for the Play-Off final. It was an especially bold line given that Widnes have won League titles, Challenge Cups and Premierships - not to mention World and European club titles.

But it was true. With the drawbridge on automatic promotion being pulled up and the franchise lottery about to grip Rugby League a win over Castleford was essential for the Vikings future.

Unfortunately that phenomenal pressure was all too much. As Widnes seized up it was the Tigers that seized the day and can now look forward to an almost guaranteed Super League future. Within 48 hours of course Widnes were in administration and the prospects of us rejoining the anointed ranks of Super League clubs had seemingly disappeared over the horizon.

But as the events of the last few weeks have shown it was not all doom and gloom, and neither was Widnes's season in 2007.

As the BBC Rugby League editor I had taken plenty of stick from my Widnes mates for choosing the Vikings 4th Round Challenge Cup tie against Wigan to be played on the Sunday for TV- just four days before our vital league opener against Leigh.

It proved a master stroke though as the Vikings brave and skilful performance against Brian Noble's side set the benchmark for a great first half of the season. Leigh were dispatched in style four days later and main rivals Castleford were also hammered as the Vikings swept all before them.

This dreamy period climaxed on a summer's day in Blackpool as Widnes whitewashed Whitehaven to bring home the Northern Rail Cup.

The joy of the Widnes fans that day should be remembered by us all as everyone now has to rally around coach Steve Mc-

Cormack and new owner Steve O'Connor to try and ensure Widnes are given the golden prize of a Super League franchise in June.

Whether this comes or not season 2007 will be remembered as a roller coaster ride for all Vikings fans – joy and despair in equal measures. And we should remember such seasons fondly for the fight to come to maintain the future of the club we all love.

Carl Hicks
BBC Rugby League Editor

To cut a long story short, 2007 was certainly a season to remember, both on and off the pitch, for the Widnes Vikings.

However, in a season full of highs and lows, one always tries to erase the negative memories, but by the same token, keep the good times permanently etched on the brain, and with the latter in mind, I have to admit that although there were plenty of moments to savour last year, and a genuine feel-good spirit among both the players, staff and spectators, which always makes my job far easier, I would like to pay tribute to one man, and that man, is none other than Steve McCormack.

Now, as an outsider looking in, one can only presume that life as a coach must be hard, both mentally and physically, with the obvious demands that it brings with it, so how Steve McCormack's head of hair has remained 'grey-free' in his career thus far, is an absolute miracle, unless he goes to the same barber as a certain Eddie Hemmings of course, which could explain it!

Back to the script though, and with Mr. McCormack it's obviously been a case of black cats crossing his path, walking under ladders or breaking mirrors for this poor bloke, because what else could be the answer for his rotten luck with these end-of-season Grand Final games.

Speaking to him before the most recent of these events at Leeds Rhinos' Headingley Carnegie Stadium, with tongue firmly in-cheek, I reminded him that, "Fourth time lucky!" had a certain ring to it, to which he agreed, but little did either of us realise at that stage, that we would be adding another digit to that particular statistic before the end of the evening.

But, that's irony for you!

Alas, all of that is behind us now, and while we can't change history we can create it, and with a lot of hard work and no doubt a little bit of luck along the way too, the future looks bright for the Widnes Vikings club, and I for one, can't wait for the 2008 season to arrive. So, as they say at the fairground when it's your turn to ride the rollercoaster, "Pay your money, sit down, get your safety belt firmly secured, and away we go!"

With Steve at the helm, we have a person who I genuinely believe is the main reason for the turnaround in attitude and professionalism at the club that we have seen in recent years, and without a doubt, he is playing a leading part in steering Widnes back in the right direction, with destination 'Promised Land' firmly in his sights.

It goes without saying, that he can't do it on his own though, and without wishing to turn this into a Party Political Broadcast, it's important that we get behind him and his team, and if we all pull together, you never know, even more good times could be just around the corner!

Mark Naughton
Rugby League Broadcaster & Commentator

In 1959 a couple in their twenties, he a journalist, she an employee of Pilkington Brothers, the famous St Helens glass manufacturers, decided that their first marital home would be in Widnes.

The decision caused some surprise, since the town was renowned, even slightly notorious, for the variety of aromas, some would bluntly call them stinks, which ascended from the Widnes Chimneys. The town's prosperity depended upon its chemical industries, and its rugby team were nicknamed the Chemics in those days. Sheila hails from Barrow, my own roots were in Newton-le-Willows, and the choice of Widnes was purely a professional one as I was developing a broadcasting career. I did not drive in those days so I travelled to the Look North Studios and BBC radio studios in Manchester and Liverpool from Farnworth, later Widnes North station, a 10-minute walk across the Wade Deacon School playing fields from our bungalow in Woodland Avenue. My career was to take me to Yorkshire, Border and Granada TV and several local stations but we stayed in Widnes for 21 years, were warmly accepted by excellent neighbours and friends, and became adopted Widnesians.

You are by now no doubt wondering where this rambling introduction is going. Simply this. When the rugby league club from just a few hundred yards down Lowerhouse Lane went into Administration shortly after the end of a dramatic roller-coaster season, the shock hit me between the eyes. I just could not believe that the club from my adopted home town, the black and whites, the chemics, who had dominated the 70's and 80's as Wigan did later, and St Helens do now, had collapsed and was in danger of going out of existence. It was just not possible.

After all, despite the fact that they had, temporarily we thought, dropped out of Super League, they had reached the divisional Grand Final, and had earlier won the Northern Rail Cup. Gates had not been brilliant, but at around an average of 3,300 they were considerably higher than say, Rochdale, Oldham and Leigh. Where had it all gone wrong ?

When, earlier in the season, I shared a couple of commentary games with Ray French and John Lawless for Radio Merseyside there was no hint of what was to come. The Chemics, sorry, Vikings, had won the matches comfortably, and were on the way back to Super League, or so we thought.

The rest is sad history. Although the Northern Rail Cup had been won, it became obvious to everyone except the most naïve and partisan supporter that Castleford had the superior squad, and the embarrassing anti-climax in the Grand Final was all too predictable long before the game was played.

Shortly after the Administration bombshell dropped I went to the splendid new Halton Stadium (I still make the slip of the tongue 'Naughton Park') and found its offices virtually deserted with a handful of anxious staff trying to put on brave faces. I have no knowledge of, or authority to speak about exactly what went wrong, although the scurrilous rumour went the rounds that the previous regime's Plan A was to get back to Super league and the Sky pot of gold, but there did nor appear to be a Plan B, if it all went wrong. Thankfully, rescue was at hand in the shape of Steve O'Connor, a man with impeccable Widnes credentials and the financial and administrative clout to back up his local loyalty and ambitions.

As an experienced and hard-headed businessman Steve knows that financial rescue with a stable and experienced administration, and a fine stadium are not in themselves guarantees of revival and a successful drive towards Super League.

Last season's squad looked good enough on paper, but too many players, some with solid reputations, did not perform when it really mattered, particularly in the bedrock area of defence. Neighbours and rivals Warrington have illustrated the fact that scoring 30-odd points with skilful attack is of no use when the opposition rattles up 32. Steve McCormack needs to spend and recruit wisely, and choose not on reputation but on performance, particularly in the painful hard graft area of tackling. it is not an enviable task, but if it brings promotion and an eventual place in a revamped Super League, here is one person who will feel, to coin again the oldest of clichés, that Widnes are back where they belong.

Keith Macklin
Radio & TV Rugby League Commentator

CHAPTER NINE

Administration

Following the defeat at Headingley rumours were rife about the future of the Club, with all kinds of rational and irrational comments and accusations being made. The existing Board of Directors had done a sterling job to keep the Club afloat since early April, but it seemed to be an open secret that the Club's financial affairs were still far from healthy, and there were now rumours of entering Administration.

Maybe promotion to Super League would have attracted a 'benefactor' to solve the problems; maybe it would have just papered over the cracks of the underlying causes of those problems. However that option was no longer available and after a necessary, but uncomfortable silence, the Chief Executive issued the following statement on 9th October on behalf of the Board of Directors:

> Following Sunday's disappointing defeat in the National League 1 Grand Final the Board met at length on Monday and Tuesday to discuss the current financial position of the Club.

After these meetings the decision was regrettably taken to put Widnes Rugby League Football Club Ltd into administration with effect from today, Tuesday 9th October, 2007.

The Board took this decision following independent advice received from Jonathan Avery-Gee, Senior Partner of Kay Johnson Gee, Chartered Accountants, who was appointed as the Administrator.

This decision will hopefully allow the Administrator the opportunity to achieve a sale of the Club and with it the potential to keep professional rugby league alive in the Borough where it has been an integral part of many people's lives for five generations and given great enjoyment.

It is a very sad time for all concerned within the Club and the Board would like to thank everybody who has contributed to its success over the years at whatever level.

The Administrator is now responsible for all matters concerning the Club. He will be seeking offers for the Club and already members of the Board have confirmed their intention to put together a package to take the Club forward into 2008 and beyond.

Pete Barrow
Chief Executive

Although it had been widely known that there were financial difficulties the fans were naturally very concerned about the future of their club following the dramatic announcement from the Chief Executive. Virtually the whole season had been played out against a backdrop of financial insecurity, with various parties making claim and counter-claim as to the root cause. I personally share the view that had a greater level of speculative investment been made in the playing staff prior to the second season in Super League, the current problems may well have been averted. Two quality signings at that time, on the back of a seventh place finish the year before, would have seen a growth in season ticket sales and other revenue streams which could have been the springboard for further continued success and growth.

In the lead up to the 2007 Grand Final rumours had been circulating that defeat would herald a 'part-time' playing staff for 2008 - indeed I was told this by a Yorkshire based Super League player just seven days before the Final - and an obvious exodus of key players. It is doubtful however, that anyone outside the boardroom had any inkling, that financially it was a case of 'Super League or bust' as we took our places at Headingley. The playing staff were certainly, in my view correctly, unaware of the situation as they took to the field at Headingley. My information is that Steve McCormack and his skipper, Mark Smith, were informed on the morning of the 9th October, and the rest of the players during the course of the 9th and 10th. As a number of the players were away on international duty with England, Scotland, Ireland and Wales it naturally took a day or two to get in touch with all of them. As mentioned previously Toa Kohe-Love had told Steven Kelly of the Runcorn & Widnes World that the first indication that the playing staff had of the seriousness of the situation was "when we were called in to sign some forms" the following week.

In order to gain an understanding of the events that ultimately led to the unhappy ending to the 2007 season I took the opportunity to discuss the club's demise with former Chairman Peter Knowles.

To put current events into perspective Mr Knowles first turned his thoughts back to the day that he became a Director of the club, and admitted that "Becoming a Director of Widnes Vikings was possibly the worst and most expensive decision I have ever made. But the decision was made from the heart not the head". It was at the end of 2005 following the resignation of five Directors, and after almost 60 years of being a Widnes supporter, that Mr Knowles "decided to put myself forward to join the Vikings Board of Directors", and was elected onto the Board at the same time as Lol Ogburn and Stephen Vaughan. "I was recently retired and had enough business experience to believe that I could help the club to move forward". At about this time Pete Barrow, who had recently joined the club as Financial Controller, started to identify that the club had serious financial problems "and as the months went by it was very clear that the club had been running with a significant deficit in its trading operations for some time".

Within a short period of time Stephen Vaughan took over from Tony Chambers as Chairman, appointing Pete Barrow as Chief Executive, and the new Chairman started to bankroll the club. Ultimately Chambers, Tom Fleet, Alan Gregson and Graham Ashton resigned from the board.

Summing up the disappointing 2006 season Mr Knowles said "We had a difficult start but the performances on the field improved as the season progressed and after Steve Mc-Cormack started to put together his own squad. But in the end we were no match for Hull KR and were beaten in the play off final. Off the field the financial problems continued. The attendances we were getting were disappointing and this combined with the low level of sponsorship we were attracting, and the costs of playing at the stadium, was resulting in us continuing to trade at a significant loss".

Whilst the catastrophic end to the 2007 season is now a

matter of record Mr Knowles admitted that "We went in to the 2007 season with some optimism, we believed we had a stronger squad than 2006 and believed we had an excellent chance of winning the play off final and gaining promotion to Super League. We also had, in Stephen Vaughan, a wealthy Chairman who was supporting the club financially".

The former chairman went on to highlight further frustrations in saying that "Considering that we started the season so successfully and were playing some excellent football it was disappointing that attendances were lower than 2006, sponsorship was also very disappointing and therefore we were still trading at a significant loss".

It is plain therefore that the two major income steams - sponsorship and 'gate receipts' - were not providing adequate levels of income to support the operating costs of the club, and this may be seen as giving some validity to the fans' oft-mentioned criticism of the club's commercial and marketing operations. Certainly with Widnes' high level of exposure, especially from Sky's live coverage of the National Leagues, I would have expected a significant level of sponsorship to be forthcoming. More worrying though was the apparent apathy displayed by the population of this 'rugby town'. Generally speaking fans will turn out in high numbers to watch their team, in any sport, as long as it is winning. It is truly remarkable then that a team not only winning, but winning in style, could not attract more fans to the Halton Stadium.

So while the club was taking major strides forward on the pitch, these were counter-balanced by the on-going and growing problems behind the scenes, which were exacerbated by the mid-season resignation of Stephen Vaughan as Chairman.

Mr Knowles conceded that having lost the financial backing of Mr Vaughan "we knew we had significant financial problems and debated whether we should go into administration at that point". This drastic action was averted at a hurriedly arranged meeting of the four remaining Directors, when "Jim Quinn and Sam Evans stated that they would support the club financially for the rest of the 2007 season as we thought we had a good chance of winning the Grand Final and getting into Super League. At the same meeting, asked by Jim Quinn and Sam Evans to take over as acting Chairman, Mr Knowles "reluctantly agreed to this in order to support Jim and Sam who had been Directors for many years and had provided financial support to the club throughout that time".

The revised Board of Directors therefore elected to keep the club going until the end of the season with the hope that promotion to Super League would attract, in the words of Mr Knowles, "new investors, new and considerably improved levels of sponsorship and increased attendances in addition to the money from Sky" and enable them to develop a business plan which would make the club sustainable.

"Jim and Sam continued to finance the club", said Mr Knowles, "both making significant personal contributions month by month. We went into the end of the season with debts that we were carrying forward but believed that if successful in the Play Off final we could overcome these. The resulting loss in the Grand Final was a bitter blow".

Aware of the implications of defeat the Directors had arranged a Board meeting for the following Tuesday to determine the best way forward for the club. However they were overtaken by events when, shortly after 9:00am on Monday 8th October, a 'fax' was received from Her Majesty's Revenue & Customs in which they reversed an offset arrangement that had been in place for over a year and demanded an immediate settlement. Failure to comply would result in a winding up order against the company. This was "the final nail in the coffin", added Mr Knowles. "We had no alternative but to seek advice from a senior insolvency practitioner."

"We met the adviser, Jonathan Avery-Gee, on Monday 8th October and when he examined the situation he told us that legally we had no alternative but to go into administration with immediate effect".

As an unwelcome adjunct to the financial situation at the club there had been rumours circulating during the final weeks of the season regarding players' pay and commitment. The issue of 'splits' and 'disquiet' in the dressing room have already been dealt with in my interviews with Steve McCormack and the 'famous five', and the rumours regarding pay can now happily also be put to bed. Mr Knowles confirmed that "Until the end of September all of the staff, both playing and non-playing, had been paid every penny that was due to them". Payments that were due to staff after that time are explained later in this chapter.

It should also be noted, however, that from the morning of the 9th October the club was in Administration and the players, and other staff, were in fact employed by the Administrator, and not Widnes Rugby League Club Ltd.

In retrospect the writing was probably on the wall when the club only made contract offers for 2008 based on attaining promotion to Super League, whereas twelve months previously 'dual contracts' were on offer for Super League or National League status. However once the club had entered Administration all contracts of employment became null and void, and as it was obviously precluded from making contract offers to players, the vultures began to hover over an uncertain Widnes playing staff. In the immediate aftermath fans took solace from the lack of instant departures of players, but this became a false dawn when within a few days other clubs slowly but surely began to proudly announce their rich pickings from the Vikings.

One surprising, but welcome omission from the list of early departures was Mark Smith. Most of us had feared that he would be one of those most in demand, and it was surprising that Mark was among those who had been left in limbo as a consequence of the post-final events.

Speaking to the Runcorn & Widnes World the popular skipper admitted that "It is a very worrying situation. Last season I had a number of clubs interested, but I have not had anything this year - even from Widnes. By this time next week I could be signing on the dole and I have a wife and child to think about. I feel for them more than myself."

Taking time to think of others he hoped that the bulk of the squad that had lifted the club's first trophy in six years could be kept together, explaining: "It would be nice to see the club offer a bit of something to the lads so they can still have a life in rugby league. I have never played with such a good bunch of lads. There were no cliques and we all got on really well." The popular 'Smithy' also spoke out in defence of the club's Directors by adding "I cannot fault the board and I know they will be doing this for the right reasons."

Among the first ex-players to speak out was Terry O'Connor who had finished his playing career, with his home-town team, just 12 months previously. "Absolutely gutted" to see the club in Administration O'Connor said it was "shocking to see the way the club has gone. Losing again in the Grand Final for the second year in a row was bad enough, but this just adds to the misery of everyone at the club.

Echoing the thoughts of many fans he added that "the town is known for its Rugby League.... there were times when every lad was playing rugby at night."

"I thought getting relegated was the lowest point of my career, but this isn't far off. Being a Widnes lad, there is nothing more heart-breaking. I am absolutely gutted."

Others to comment included Martin Offiah and Jonathan Davies, members of the "Chemics" World Club Championship winning team of 1989. While Offiah found it "a sad demise of what is still a great club" where he had enjoyed "great times," he felt that keeping "players on full time contracts.....is a gamble and it obviously hasn't paid off."

Team-mate Davies added "It is very sad. I had some very good times at Widnes. Both the club and the fans were superb, so to see the club in this position is very, very disappointing indeed."

Whilst the protocols of Administration meant that technically the club ceased to exist from 9th October 2007, and the business was being run by the Administrator, there was necessarily limited news or comment emanating from within the Halton Stadium. Ironically it was this lack of communication with the fans, and the frustration that it engendered, that was to fan the flames of speculation as every half-truth or rumour was readily accepted as fact by 'news hungry' supporters.

Throughout this period of uncertainty the only hard facts that came into the public domain, through a variety of external web-sites, concerned the increasing flow of players who were leaving the Vikings to join clubs that would be our main rivals in 2008 - assuming that the RFL would grant the new owners a licence to compete in National League One. To make matters worse the rumours linking Steve McCormack to coaching vacancies at other clubs were beginning to gain momentum.

Although understanding that there were strict procedures to be followed fans were understandably becoming more and more frustrated as time wore on without any sign of progress or official comment. The harsh truth of the situation was that whilst the Administrator was charged with the responsibility of finding new owners, the fans were forced to watch their favourite players moving to pastures new, with no immediate likelihood of being able to retain or recruit for 2008.

However, on 17th October, there appeared to be some progress and cause for optimism when the Administrator, Mr Jonathan Avery-Gee issued the following statement:

I have currently received expressions of interest from two parties with regards to the purchase of the Club. Both interested parties have been requested to produce an opening balance sheet, detailed profit and loss account and cash-flow statement. To date neither party has supplied this information although one party is well on the way to doing so.

When this information is received it has to be presented to both the Rugby Football League and the landlord, Halton Borough Council, to establish whether they consider the parties to be acceptable to them to take the Club forward.

Jonathan Avery-Gee
Administrator

Within a couple of days of this announcement one of the consortia had 'gone public' and held an open meeting to publicise their plans to secure the future of Widnes Vikings. In excess of 100 fans heard members of the consortium outline their proposals, adding that they had already secured new sponsorship revenue, lined up 24 players and spoken to potential coaches.

Naturally at such an early stage it was not possible for the prospective new owners to publicise hard facts such as financial input or the names of potential signings or appointments. This, and an unrealistic expectation of 'hard news' on the part of some people, led to a mixed reception as the fans still waited to learn the identity of the club's new owners. The speculation and concern about the ownership issue - and indeed the survival of the club - was to rumble on for a seemingly inordinate amount of time. However when the new owners were finally announced on 1st November, it should be remembered that this was just 23 days after entering Administration.

In the meantime another piece of unwelcome news came when the following statement was released by the club on 23rd October:

> Vikings Head Coach Steve McCormack is to leave the Club. The popular 34 year old has decided to resign from the position he has held for the last two seasons.
>
> Speaking about his decision McCormack said, "It has been a challenging and enjoyable two years at Widnes and I am sad to leave. However, with all the off the field changes currently taking place I feel that it is in the best interests of all parties to have a fresh start in 2008. I would like to take this opportunity to thank everyone at the Club and all the fans for their support over the last two seasons and wish them every success for the forthcoming season."

As with coaches in all sports fans have divided opinions about their abilities unless their team is winning trophies every year. Whilst this was also true of Steve McCormack - he had suffered irrational abuse from a small minority during 2006 - it is true to say that he had won over all but a handful during 2007. This he managed to do through a combination of his team's performances and his own personality and willingness to speak to the fans.

More bad news was to come when, within 24 hours of the announcement of his departure, it was confirmed that not only had McCormack accepted an offer to join Hull KR as an assistant to Justin Morgan, but that double record holder Mick Nanyn had left for NL2 Oldham! Whilst it was understandable for McCormack to accept the role with a Super League club, fans were totally bemused by Nanyn's move to Oldham. It was widely anticipated that the free-scoring centre would be a target for the top teams in NL1 or even some Super League outfits, but the move to Boundary Park was a real shock which only served to heighten the sense of frustration felt by the fans.

While at this point there were still some members of the 2007 squad who had not signed for other clubs, there was now great fear among supporters that the departure of the Head Coach and the talismanic Nanyn would finally lead to the floodgates opening.

The passing of every additional day as a 'rudderless ship' meant that the club, constrained by its inability to make any positive, concrete moves for the new season and beyond, was drifting further away from its target of Super League status. Although secondary to the survival of the club, the thorny question of a bid for a Super League Licence for 2009 still occupied many people's minds. In some quarters it was felt that recent events had wrecked any hope of gaining a Licence, along with the belief that Celtic Crusaders and Salford were virtually 'shoo-ins' for the anticipated two additional places for 2009. In contrast some were still pinning their hopes on the fact that a financial 'clean sheet' might in fact strengthen the bid, and this seemed to be borne out by the fact that amidst all the speculation the club had re-iterated its intention to pursue a Licence bid after new owners had been identified.

Of more immediate concern, however, were the questions of survival and whether the new club could muster a squad strong enough to overcome the expected points penalty levied by the RFL, and survive in National League One. However on

25th October there was the hint of positive news to come in the near future when Chief Executive Pete Barrow issued the following statement:

Since going into administration the staff at the Club have been working for the Administrator.

They are preparing for submission to him a business plan for next year accompanied by a detailed budget which reflects fully the financial implications of that plan. The finances of the club has meant that some areas of activity have necessarily been reduced or postponed but careful consideration has been given to maintain a balance within all aspects of the club.

The budget must identify a profit or at very least break even thereby demonstrating that the Club can go forward as a viable business venture. The Administrator must be satisfied of this position then he will consider any offers for the club/business. The financial position will be one of a number of criteria he is legally bound to consider in making this decision.

Timescale for completion is late this week with a view to a decision being made early next week. The budget and business plan will be completed and submitted by the end of this week.

The Administrator expects to make a decision on new owners in the early part of next week.

Pete Barrow
Chief Executive

As the pace finally seemed to be quickening towards the anticipated announcement from the Administrator local MP Derek Twigg voiced his support of the club when making the following statement:

> I share the concerns of the whole community about the plight of Widnes Vikings. As a long standing supporter and sponsor I know how important the Club is to the local community.
>
> I have already discussed the situation with Halton Borough Council, the Administrator and the Rugby Football League (RFL). It is clear that everyone is working hard to find a solution that would see the Club back on its feet again.
>
> I was very heartened by my discussions with Richard Lewis, Chief Executive at the RFL who has told me the RFL will be as helpful and flexible as they can be within the rules.
>
> I will continue to do all I can to help and I am already in the process of contacting some local businesses about what help they can give.
>
> Derek Twigg MP

It was plain to see that there was a ground-swell of support for the club across the local community and beyond. In addition to the support of 'the fan in the street', the Local Authority and the local Member of Parliament, supporters of neighbouring Super League clubs took the trouble to identify themselves as they offered their support and contributed to the various fund-raising schemes operating in the town.

But despite the re-assuring pledges of support and press releases from various quarters the hard-core fans were still anxiously awaiting positive news about a new owner. Then, on 1st November, in what some would call typical Widnes fashion, the hearts and minds of those fans were first tossed into turmoil, and then within hours saw the light at the end of the tunnel.

Against the ever-present background of speculation and rumour two announcements were made via the official club website. During the morning the following information was released:

> Following a meeting with Halton Borough Council on Wednesday evening, the bid for the Club led by Jim Quinn and Sam Evans has reluctantly been withdrawn.

> Both will continue to support the Club and wish it well into the future.

> The Administrator is continuing to liaise with the Club on the bids remaining on the table.

But as the day unfolded this apparent setback gave way to anticipation that there would finally be a definitive announcement later in the day. And so it proved when at 8.00pm the statement that all Widnes fan's had been longing for appeared on the web-site to herald a new era for Widnes Vikings:

> Widnes businessman Steve O'Connor has purchased the assets of Widnes Rugby League Club Ltd from the Administrator.

> Mr O'Connor mounted a rescue operation to save the ailing club after it narrowly failed to win promotion to the Super League this season.

Crippled by debts and with an exodus of star players, the historic club's future looked bleak as it was placed into administration.

But now Mr O'Connor, in partnership with Halton Borough Council, has devised a business plan that guarantees the future of Rugby League in Widnes.

Mr O'Connor, a familiar and respected figure in the Halton business community, recently sold his shares in his highly-successful Widnes-based rail freight and logistics company, O'Connor Group, to Stobart Group in a multi-million pound deal.

He is now responsible for developing the Stobart's brand across the North West.

Initially he has pledged £250,000 to guarantee the immediate future of the club, which will trade as a new company, on top of a five figure sum he paid to secure the rights of the Widnes Vikings' brand.

Now Mr O'Connor and Halton Borough Council Chief Executive David Parr will undertake a complete overhaul of the entire operation to ensure the long-term future viability of the club which plays its matches in the council-owned Halton Stadium.

Father-of-three Mr O'Connor, 42, a self-confessed football fan, who lives in Frodsham, Cheshire, says he decided to purchase Widnes Vikings to ensure the club is run by successful and experienced business people, committed to the local community.

He said: "I would be the first to admit that football is my first love rather than Rugby League but ultimately I am fiercely passionate about sport and I'm equally passionate about business and the community where I was brought up.

"What has happened to Widnes Rugby League Club over recent years is a tragedy. It's a fantastic institution which should be competing at the very highest level.

"I firmly believe that, with the support of Halton Borough Council, I can put together a team of experienced individuals from the world of business to work alongside talented and successful rugby people to ensure we can bring the glory days back to Widnes.

"My goal is to use my wealth and expertise to help put strong foundations in place where Widnes Vikings can flourish and take their rightful place in the Super League elite where they belong."

Over the next few days Mr O'Connor, Mr Parr and their advisors will meet senior officials at the Rugby Football League headquarters in Leeds to outline their short-term proposals for the club and their longer-term vision.

Mr O'Connor said: "I fully understand the passion, commitment and desire of the supporters who want to see this rugby club move forward and I want to see their wishes fulfilled.

"I appreciate the public will want to know all the details about our plans. However, we have had to move extremely swiftly to complete this deal and it is too soon to talk publicly in detail about our long-term proposals.

"At the moment it is important to reassure the people who work behind the scenes at the club, those players we are looking to bring to Widnes Vikings and the fans that the club's future is in safe hands.

"Much work needs to be carried out to put a management structure in place for the forthcoming season and to develop a strategy to ensure our place in the Super League by 2009.

"As soon as we are in a position to give more details, the dedicated fans of Widnes Vikings will be first to know."

With the Local Authority holding a 19% stake in the new company (later confirmed as Widnes Sport Company Ltd), Leader of the Council, Councillor Tony McDermott added:

"Over the past few weeks we have spent many hours talking to a variety of consortiums to try and find a solution. We were very impressed with the proposal submitted by Steve O'Connor. "His proposal offers a substantial cash injection and impressive long-term vision – but at the same time recognises the short-term challenges required to put Widnes Vikings back together again.

"We are now working in partnership with Steve to ensure that the future of Rugby League in Halton is secure and Widnes Vikings can once again challenge for Super League status."

It later emerged that being embarrassed by the parlous state of the former World Club Champions had driven Mr O'Connor to instigate the process that eventually led to the ownership of his local club. Finding himself in the fortunate position where he could make an investment, Mr O'Connor sought talks with the Council with a view to helping to put the club back on the right path.

Whilst his original intention was to make a donation or set up a trust, in conjunction with other like-minded local businessmen, the lack of support persuaded him to forge head in partnership with the Council.

The new Vikings owner admitted that such a venture could not be described as a sound financial investment, but added that a 'corporate strategy would be put in place, together with realistic goals and objectives, and fallback targets'. In a strange way talk of 'fallback targets' was seen as a positive indicator by the majority of the club's supporters as this indicated that not only did Mr O'Connor have a 'Plan A' but there was also a 'Plan B'. There would be no boom or bust approach to re-awaken this 'sleeping giant'!

During the passage of the twenty three long, dark days of Administration there had been a great deal of concern, and frustration, expressed by Vikings fans as they searched for any crumb of information that might give them hope. They were, in the main, unaware of what was happening behind closed doors to their club.

Following an interview with a representative of the Manchester based Chartered Accountants Kay Johnson Gee - the Administrators - I am able to set out below some of the facts surrounding that process.

Following the Grand Final defeat, and the subsequent demand from HMRC, Mr Jonathan Avery-Gee was asked to carry out an independent assessment of the financial situation of the club, and report back to the Board of Directors. His conclusion, underlined by the loss of £800,000 potential income from Sky Television, was that the club 'were unable to meet their liabilities when they were due'.

It is now a matter of record that at the Board Meeting held on Monday 8th October 2007 the Club's Directors voted to place the club into Administration.

At that meeting the Directors considered the advice of Mr Avery-Gee, and explored all options open to them for the continuance of the club. The main thrust of Mr Avery-Gee's advice was that the club had significant debts with little or no assets with which to offset those liabilities. Widnes Rugby League Club Ltd had liabilities approaching £1.5 million, with the major creditors and approximate amounts being:

HMRC (VAT and Inland Revenue)	£590,000
Halton Borough Council	£329,000
Directors & Shareholders	£337,000
Trade & Expense Creditors	£143,000
Staff holiday pay *	£50,000

The company's assets were identified as:

Exercise & Medical equipment
Fixtures & Fittings
Motor Vehicle
Computer equipment
Residual Club Shop stock

*   As a consequence of the timing of the rugby league season it is a contractual obligation that holidays are taken during October and November and, following Administration, this became a liability to the company. The figure quoted represents the 'preferential element' paid to individuals by the Government funded Redundancy Payments Office.

With the liabilities far outstripping the assets there was no 'book value' for the club and in fact the most valuable, or saleable, part of the club was its 'Goodwill'. This left only two possible outcomes - Administration or Liquidation - for the company (club), particularly as there was a real possibility of HMRC seeking a winding up order against the company.

With the decision taken to place the company into Administration the necessary documents were sworn at 6.30pm, and lodged with the Manchester District Registry on the morning of 9th October 2007. From that point the club was effectively being run by the Administrator, Mr Jonathan Avery-Gee, Senior Partner of Kay Johnson Gee.

In the days and weeks that followed this shocking announcement there had been debate locally about the necessity of the club going into Administration. There was a school of thought that it could have survived without taking such drastic action. However, with the purpose of Administration being 'to find a better realisation than if a company is wound up' (liquidated), there seem, to me, to be two compelling reasons to support the move into Administration:

i)   'Winding up' orders cannot be instigated against a company that is in Administration.

ii)   A company that has been wound up, or liquidated, ceases trading, and is a much less attractive proposition to any purchaser.

The obvious benefit of the first is that it forestalls any likelihood of the second taking place, at least until the Administrator has exhausted all possibilities of selling the business as a going concern. If Widnes Rugby League Club Ltd had in fact ceased trading it would have been much more difficult to find a saviour such as Steve O'Connor, and therefore more difficult to satisfy the requirements of Halton Borough Council and the RFL. The likely scenario would most probably have been the end of professional rugby league in the town !

The reality of the situation was that the club was insolvent and the rescue operation was underway in the hands of the Administrator, whose task was to achieve the following:

1)   rescue the company as a 'going concern'

2)   achieve a better result for the company's creditors as a whole than would be likely if the company were wound up (without first being in Administration).

3)   realise property in order to make a distribution to one or more secured or preferential creditors.

The first stage in this process was for the Administrator to appoint an Agent to undertake the task of identifying prospective purchasers of WRLC Ltd. Once potential owners had been identified the Administrator then held meetings with each of the interested parties to assess the viability of their bids, based on cashflow and business plan projections, before submission to Halton Borough Council and the RFL for approval.

Whilst it is normal practice to recommend that the company is sold to the highest bidder, there can be conditions placed upon a sale. In this case Halton Borough Council (as landlord), and the RFL (as the governing body who issue the licence to compete) set a condition that the club should not be sold to any person(s) who had been involved in the previous management of the club, effectively ruling out former Board members.

Eventually the sale to Steve O'Connor was approved and he was granted a licence to run the club for 3 months, whilst it technically remained in Administration. Once approval had been received from the RFL Steve O'Connor would be able to assume full ownership, and the Administrator move to discharge the Administration Order and dissolve the old company.

The Club had been in limbo since entering Administration on 9th October with the fans desperate for a saviour as it appeared to lurch towards possible extinction. In little more than three weeks it now appeared that the future of the club had been safeguarded - by an owner with what many saw as the dream ticket - strong business credentials and an allegiance to the local community.

Every ending has a new beginning, and with such a positive, and decisive, leader at the helm the Vikings may yet be setting sail for the 'promised land' in 2009.

CHAPTER TEN

A New Beginning

It is true to say that the fans were both surprised and impressed by the speed with which Mr O'Connor took action, as in less than 24 hours he demonstrated his determination and resourcefulness to take the Vikings back to the top level of the domestic game.

Since his departure there had been much debate and speculation surrounding the identity of Steve McCormack's replacement, with Karl Harrison leading the way from Ian Millward and Neil Kelly in most polls.

In announcing the sudden return of McCormack, Steve O'Connor had managed to completely wrong-foot the media and fans alike, and at a stroke re-kindle optimism and expectation among the clubs supporters. Describing his Head Coach as 'driven' and 'very bright', with the 'respect of players' Mr O'Connor cited the need for stability and the fact that in 2007, with little direction, McCormack had put together 'a very successful side'.

Resuming duties at the Halton Stadium just 9 days after his departure McCormack said: "I'm absolutely delighted to be back with Widnes and to have the opportunity to take the Vikings on to even greater success in the future. When I recently announced my reluctant departure from the club it came at a time when I genuinely felt I'd taken them as far as possible under the Vikings' existing structure.

"With the change of ownership – and the new financial structure of the club – I believe this is a fantastic time to be involved with the Vikings. Knowing the many strengths of the club, the unrivalled devotion of its fans plus the commitment shown by Steve O'Connor, I just couldn't resist the opportunity to get back in charge. The Vikings really are on the march again!"

Acknowledging the Directors of Hull KR "for their understanding in allowing Steve McCormack to return to the Vikings so soon after joining Hull" Mr O'Connor added: "Steve McCormack has done a tremendous job at Widnes over the past couple of seasons in very difficult circumstances. I'm convinced he's the right man to take the club into the Super League and we will provide him with the resources necessary to challenge for the very top honours. Steve knows the club, is popular with the fans and has the ability and experience to make this club great again. Steve's appointment is just the first important step to secure the future of this club. I'm working around-the-clock to develop our business plan and intend to share my vision with the Vikings' greatest asset – our supporters – over the coming weeks."

The Leader of Halton Borough Council, Cllr Tony McDermott, also spoke out in support of the re-appointment of Steve McCormack by adding "Steve has a proven track record and is well respected in the game by players and officials. Steve's return offers a real opportunity to take the Vikings back to the Super League. We are looking forward to working with him."

Further encouragement came with the news that the antic-ipated move to a part-time playing staff would not take place, and McCormack would be able to operate with a full-time squad. Welcoming this decision the Head Coach commented that: "The Co-operative National League is a fiercely competi-tive and highly intensive championship. To compete success-fully at this level it is important the team is run on a full-time basis which helps me immensely in attracting the right calibre of experienced players to the club. Steve O'Connor's announcement is a massive boost for the club. Within min-utes of the announcement of my appointment as Head Coach, players from England and overseas were ringing me express-ing interest in joining Widnes Vikings. There's a monumental amount of work to be done but already you can sense the buzz of excitement and expectation and everyone is now looking forward to the new season."

As mentioned previously, under the terms and procedures of Administration Mr O'Connor was at this stage in fact run-ning the company 'under licence' pending the granting of his 'full ownership'. This allowed him a period of 3 months to satisfy all requirements that may be laid down by the RFL be-fore full ownership could be ratified. So, with the Head Coach safely in place Mr O'Connor was able to turn his attention to the vital meeting with the RFL and gaining their approval of his vision and proposals for the future of the club. This was the beginning of a process through which the club re-applied for membership of the governing body and to be re-admitted to NL1 for the coming season.

Supported by Vikings' Chief Executive Pete Barrow and the Leader of the Council, Cllr Tony McDermott, Mr O'Connor was later reported as finding the initial talks "encouraging", and being "hopeful the RFL Board will agree to our membership quickly so we can then concentrate on instigating the numerous ideas contained within the business plan to rebuild the Vikings."

The club, already recognised as having one of the best stadiums in Rugby League in addition to an award winning community programme, world class scholarship programme, and top class academy, could now add a robust commercial background to its CV. It was hoped that the impressive combination of these factors would make re-admission to the RFL little more than a formality, however it was not until 19th November that Widnes' membership of the RFL was confirmed through the following press release from Red Hall:

The RFL Board of Directors have today re-admitted the Widnes Vikings club to the co-operative National League One competition from 2008 onwards.

In accordance with the RFL Operational Rules, the Vikings' membership of the competition was suspended after the club undertook an act of insolvency and the ownership of the club changed hands at the conclusion of the 2007 season.

Also in accordance with the RFL Operational Rules the club will be deducted nine competition points with effect from the start of the 2008 co-operative National League season.

The consequence of this delay was two-fold: The surge of enthusiasm and confidence which the new ownership had brought to Vikings supporters began to wane, but more importantly Steve McCormack was unable to start building his squad until Widnes' status was confirmed.

In common with many Vikings supporters I had felt that the task of identifying suitable and viable new owners of the club would have been the biggest obstacle to overcome, but the apparent sluggishness of the RFL decision making process began to put new doubts into people's minds. On the one hand none other than RFL Executive Chairman Richard Lewis was quoted as saying that it "was good news to have them (Widnes) in full running order", whilst the lack of news coming from Red Hall was seen by some as sending out a different message. The words of the RFL Chairman had created in some quarters the belief that the club would be 'rubber-stamped' back into the fold within days if not hours, but as time wore on the messageboards came alive again as the nervousness of the previous few weeks returned.

On finally being re-admitted to the Rugby Football League Chairman Steve O'Connor commented: "We're obviously disappointed to be docked points for the start of the season but accept this as being the RFL's normal course of action following a club being placed into administration. However, we're confident we can establish a squad that can overcome this hurdle and take Vikings on to great success." He added that: "We must now move on and concentrate on our long-term plans for the revival of Widnes Vikings and to secure success in National League 1 which can act as a springboard for a successful Super League Licence application".

Widnes' application to be re-admitted as members of the Rugby Football League had triggered a standard process relating to clubs which become insolvent, or where ownership changes hands. The application was considered by the RFL Board, which comprised the Executive Chairman, Chief Executive, and three non-executive Directors, who were charged to exercise 'due diligence' in regard to the following:

i)   Any new owners of a club will safeguard the future of that club and promote rugby league at all levels in that particular area.

        This is designed to guard against speculative acquisition of a club and its assets, which may later be stripped for purely financial gain on the part of a new owner.

ii) The submission of a robust Business Plan that demonstrates that the club is sustainable.

iii) An appropriate Staffing structure exists

iv) The club is seen as part of, and involved in, its local community.

v) A positive and realistic vision and projection for the future of the club.

Whilst fans had been anxiously awaiting news from Red Hall there had been much speculation regarding the possible penalty for entering Administration, some of which centred around general misconceptions of what is in the RFL's 'rule book', and the circumstances pertaining to other recent cases.

Convincing, but ultimately erroneous, arguments were put forward for no penalty, a six point deduction, and even relegation to National League 2. Whilst those championing the case for no penalty were basing their argument on the fact that the club had completed the season prior to entering Adminstration, the 'six point' campaign was citing the recent adjudications in the cases of Doncaster and Swinton as precedents.

In fact the RFL does not differentiate between clubs who become insolvent during the season and those who find themselves in that position during the close season. The penalty structure is the same in both instances although, interestingly, there is scope under the RFL's guidelines to vary the penalty handed down according to the circumstances of each case.

With regard to the comparison with Doncaster and Swin-

ton I was informed by the RFL that their penalties were cal-
culated under the old points system of 2 points for a win, as
they "did not *enter* Administration during 2007". In all three
cases the penalty is equivalent to the points gained for winning
three matches.

So ultimately all was well as the Vikings were cleared to play
in NL1 for 2008, although they would have to overcome a 9
point penalty to achieve their immediate target of qualifying
for the end of season play-offs. In addition Steve McCormack
was at last able to begin to put his squad together and we were
soon to be cheered by the announcement of the first batch of
signings. A year previously Mark Smith had given the fans a
massive boost when, prior to the 2006 Grand Final, he was
the first player to commit himself, on a dual contract, to the
Vikings for 2007. The ever-popular 'Smithy' was to the fore
again when he and team-mates Bob Beswick, Gavin Dodd,
Dean Gaskell and local boy Paul Noone achieved instant cult
status by remaining loyal to the club during its darkest days
and re-sign for 2008 as soon as RFL rules permitted it.

Whilst waiting for the green light from Red Hall Steve
O'Connor began his task of re-building the club by issuing a
challenge to the people of Halton to come out and support the
Vikings in the new season. Citing the average attendance in
2007 of 3,300 Mr O'Connor commented "This just isn't good
enough. We are now up against the wall – we need to be very
clear – you use it or you lose it."

Hopeful of putting together a very strong case to meet
the various criteria for a Super League Licence for 2009 Mr
O'Connor emphasised that "the final piece in the jigsaw is in
the hands of the people of Halton. I hope that if any good at
all can come out of the club being forced into administration,
it is that it is a wake-up call for the whole town not to take
things for granted. We want to fill the stadium on match days

and create a unique atmosphere. The fans are an absolutely vital ingredient for success and I hope they will catch the mood of what I want to achieve here. I absolutely would not be involved with the Widnes Vikings if I didn't think the club had a successful future."

At this stage, following the tension of the Administration process, the fans' optimism was on a steep upward spiral as the new owner was making very positive comments about the future of their club. Buoyed by this new-found positivity supporters were enthusiastically looking forward to seeing the flesh on the bones of Steve O'Connor's plans.

That opportunity arose when the new chairman of Widnes Vikings arranged a Fans Forum, held at the stadium on 6th December, at which he shared the platform with fellow Board members David Parr (Chief Executive of Halton Borough Council) and Alex Bonney (Chief Executive), and Head Coach Steve McCormack. Such was the interest generated by this that within 24 hours of its announcement the evening, hosted by Steve Roberts of Radio Merseyside, had been made an all-ticket event.

Encouraged by the overwhelming response to this initiative Mr O'Connor commented: "Unfortunately we are unable to accommodate more than 450 fans on the night but will endeavour to publish a synopsis of the evening on the new-look official website".

Since the announcement of Mr O'Connor's successful bid for the club there had been much discussion, based on his business connections, about possible new sponsorship deals. Indeed this was the first question to be answered, in emphatic style, as we all approached the stadium. The sight of a fully liveried 'Eddie Stobart' vehicle outside the main entrance instantly made those attending feel that they were now part of something substantial and tangible. And once inside the sense of professionalism was all-pervading from the video 'appetiser' of yesteryear to the slick design of the new web-site.

Once the evening was under way not only did we receive confirmation that the Stobart Group was to be the shirt sponsor for the Vikings, but that the widely renowned logistics company had also secured naming rights for the stadium. For the next five years the former Naughton Park, which had 'morphed' into the AutoQuest Stadium and then Halton Stadium, would now be known as The Stobart Stadium.

Citing the new sponsorship package as "a fantastic boost for the club" and "a key part of our business plans to regenerate Widnes Vikings", Steve O'Connor expressed the need for not only the people of Widnes and Halton to support the club in numbers, but also to attract new fans from the wider local community. The club's new chairman underlined this need to improve match attendances when he pointed out that this is one of the main criteria that the RFL will consider when awarding Licences for 2009, and one that is outside his direct control.

Mr O'Connor advised the fans that, following his meeting with the RFL, he had learnt that there are five key areas to the Licence application: -

§	the stadium
§	community initiatives
§	playing strength and academies
§	a sound business plan
§	the fan base

Confident that his business team would put a powerful business proposition to the RFL he went on to say that "I believe four of these are achievable, through professional people, with the energy and enthusiasm of a driven management team

.........(but) at the end of the day it's the fans who will decide if that Super League application is successful."

Highlighting a cost of up to £1 million to put the club in a position to win a Super League Licence, Mr O'Connor added that it would be an essential part of any successful Licence application that the club could demonstrate that attendances were on an upward spiral, towards a level that could support a Super League club. So, in an attempt to boost attendances the club was seeking a more attractive pricing structure and "to create an environment that will attract families. We need to provide an entertaining package that is affordable and that mums, dads and children will want to come and watch every week". Then, in response to a question from the floor the Board took the opportunity to demonstrate its positive, and aggressive, marketing policy by announcing significant reductions in season ticket prices, in addition to cheaper match-day admission for 2008. However, it was pointed out that lower admission prices could only be sustained if there was a greater number of fans coming through the turnstiles.

Explaining the need, and desire, of all parties to succeed in this venture the Chairman pointed out that neither he, nor his partners from Halton Borough Council "can afford to be involved in this if it fails. I don't want to be associated with a business that fails.I would only have got involved if I thought we could make a success of it. We are very clear what the objectives are and what the milestones are to achieve a Super League Licence."

"We have a short window of opportunity to prove to the Rugby League that we're very serious about an application. I'm very confident that, with the support of the fans, we will deliver a very professional Super League Licence application".

Underlining the amount of work to be done Mr O'Connor stressed that "for a successful bid, this has to be a business that is capable of a £4million turnover and 10,000 people coming to the game every week. Not necessarily 10,000 people in this league – but 10,000 people to watch Super League. That's the be all and end all. If this club cannot generate 10,000 fans to watch Super League, it wouldn't be viable to make that bid. However, I'm sure we can deliver more people than historically have been coming here over the last 12 months at an average of 3,300 per game which is a long, long way from enabling us to satisfy the payroll for the business we need for next year.

Having said that, if we really struggle to hit the numbers, we might need a plan B and that seems to be what has been missing. Plan B is that we build for 2011 and that we build a successful club that is successful in applying for a licence next time around. It's not the first aspiration but we have to be realistic and not have a boom and bust mentality that it's that or nothing. It would be folly, I think".

Halton Borough Council Chief Executive, and Vikings Board member, David Parr, told fans: "Halton is a rugby league borough and the Vikings are a very important part of the community that is Widnes, that is Halton. They are at the heart of the community and certainly, when I've spoken to people, it's been pretty clear that the town needs a successful team.

"There is a lot of evidence that successful sporting clubs bring a lot of success within a town, within a borough. And certainly from the discussion I've had with local politicians, local businesses and local people – there was a big desire to ensure the Vikings survived".

Mr Parr went on to add that Mr O'Connor had pledged to enhance the key role that the club already played in providing activities for young people through its community initiatives.

It was plain to see, from Mr O'Connor's words throughout the evening, that the club was going to be run as a 'business', on business principles. "The days in which sports clubs can be run on blind faith" are, said the Vikings chairman "long gone", quoting the example of what happened to Leeds United Football Club.

Although the chairman had announced a major reduction in the price of season tickets and match day tickets for the 2008 season he warned: "The business cannot afford not to sell its product. It's a chicken and egg. We need a demonstration of people who are committed to the club. We are hoping to charge less to encourage more people to come in."

With Super League Licences being awarded in June or July Mr O'Connor re-iterated the need to "demonstrate that something dramatic has happened at Widnes since the end of last season. We have a black mark against us financially because we look like an organisation that is not sustainable, so we need to fix that and when we deliver our presentation it will be such a sensational change, if we can demonstrate an improvement in the number of people coming to the games, that they will find it very, very difficult to resist our application".

"As much as possible, I will put the financial commitment in; I will put the professional commitment in but it is absolutely down to the fans whether or not we win that application".

Mr O'Connor added: "We are looking at every aspect of the Vikings' operation to ensure the long-term future of rugby league in Widnes. This is a fresh start for the club and we wanted to develop a new, modern look in keeping with the demands of the 21st century. Widnes has a fantastic heritage and that's a great foundation to build upon. Now our aim is to bring financial stability to the club and use that as a springboard to seek a return to those glorious days, not that long ago, when the town boasted the best club side in the world".

Having outlined the general principles of how the club will

be run under his tenure, and the requirements of the RFL's Licensing process, Mr O'Connor turned his attention to the more immediate challenges that face the club.

Whilst there had been much talk of 'business principles' there was equal reference to the need for the club to be 'up to date' and to embrace the benefits of modern technology. The first evidence of this was the change of the club logo from the familiar 'viking head' to a more simplistic image based on a viking longboat. Whilst it is true that there was some resistance to the introduction of the 'on-line' purchasing of tickets and merchandise, and the new logo, they were to become more readily accepted with the passage of time. These factors, in conjunction with the launch of a new web-site and a new playing strip, were perhaps more tangible evidence of change for the fans than talk of 'business plans', and they demonstrated the dynamic style of the revitalised Widnes Vikings.

Prior to unveiling the club's new web-site Mr O'Connor took the opportunity to pay tribute to the work of Vikings fan Chris Lines who had voluntarily designed its forerunner.

During the demonstration of the new web-site it was immediately apparent that it is intended to be the fulcrum for most of the club's non-footballing operations. In addition to the traditional features the new site will also include a 'video library' and the ability to purchase match tickets, season tickets and club merchandise 'on-line'. Slick as this new operation appeared to be it did raise a concern for those without access to the internet. However while Mr O'Connor explained the demographic and cost benefits of the 'on-line' service, he reassured fans that "what you can do on the internet you can still do by contacting the club by 'phone or letter".

Finally, in little more than a month since coming out of Administration, and just over two weeks since gaining the approval of the RFL, the club were able to unveil the new playing kit for 2008. The new strips, predominantly black for the 'home' kit, and white for the 'away' version, are to be produced by market leaders Nike, and met with almost universal approval from the fans. The shirts will carry the name of 'Stobart' - one of the country's most recognisable brands - on the front, whilst the O'Connor logo is featured on the back and Halton Borough Council's will appear on the shorts.

At the end of the evening the expectant mood of fans entering the room had been replaced with one of confidence about the future of their club as they left.

In the days and weeks that followed the 'forum' Steve O'Connor's promise to build a more professional unit continued to bear fruit, as modifications to the existing office accommodation and the construction of a new fitness suite under the North Stand went hand-in-hand with the continued recruitment to the management team at the Stobart Stadium.

Having told the fans that he would create a management team which would be comprised of skilled and experienced people from the worlds of business and rugby league, Mr O'Connor's next appointments certainly bore testimony to that ideal.

Leading the way was the appointment of Mike Banks to the key role of Commercial Manager. Mr Banks, having gained a wealth of experience from senior positions in a variety of top-flight sporting organisations - including the Haydock Park based Jockey Club, Everton FC and Sale Sharks - immediately turned his attention to the twin tasks of raising the profile of the club and boosting match attendances significantly above the 2007 average of 3,300.

Commenting on his appointment Mr Banks said "I'm very excited and this is a fantastic opportunity. There's a lot of work to do but with my background I'm very confident I will make a tremendous difference. I am absolutely sure we can increase gates week on week." Echoing his chairman's thoughts on attracting, and keeping, new fans he added "We must make every game an experience for spectators and whether it's a family, individual or corporate client, we're aiming to give them a day they won't forget."

Mr Banks' appointment was followed just days later by the return of two former favourites.

Whilst it had long been rumoured that John Stankevitch would be returning to the club, in one coaching capacity or another, the appointment of Terry O'Connor took people by surprise as it involved a new position in the structure of the club. As explained on the club's web-site Terry was appointed to the new position of Sporting Director, and will be responsible for a wide range of administration duties including player recruitment, player welfare and setting up community initiatives through schools and youth groups. The former skipper will also be assisting with the Vikings' Super League Licence application as he undertakes his new duties whilst continuing with his work with Sky Sports.

Following his appointment former skipper O'Connor echoed the optimism of the fans when he said: "There's obviously a tremendous amount of work to be done to transform the fortunes of Vikings and I'm thrilled at being given the chance to help. Since Steve O'Connor took over, people within rugby league are all talking about the professionalism he has brought to Widnes. There's a genuine excitement in the town that big things are going to happen and I'm delighted to be able to be a part of it.

"I'm really looking forward to working with my great friend Steve McCormack. I'm hoping I will be able to take a lot of pressure off Steve's shoulders by looking after all the off-field activities involving the players, their welfare and offering practical support to them, leaving Steve free to concentrate all his energies on the playing side and developing a successful team."

Chairman Steve O'Connor said: "At the outset I made it clear we would transform this club by introducing experienced business professionals to work alongside talented and successful people from the world of rugby league. Terry O'Connor is ideally placed to help us achieve our goals of securing the long-term future of this club and mounting a successful campaign to win one of the coveted Super League licences."

On the same day it was also announced that John Stankevitch would be returning to the club as Assistant to Steve Mc-Cormack. 'Stanky' had built a strong reputation as coach to the Widnes Senior Academy squad before leaving to take up the Head Coach position at Doncaster in June, a position from which he had resigned in November.

As I draw a line under the events of 2007 there is a ground-swell of support for the revitalised Widnes Vikings, under the dynamic leadership of its new owners. However, it should not be forgotten that if Peter Knowles and his interim Board of Directors had not elected to keep the club afloat, following the resignation of Steven Vaughan, there may not have been a club for Steve O'Connor to rescue.

A New Beginning

From October 9th 2007 there was despair.

From November 1st 2007 there was hope.

From the Fans Forum there was a declaration of intent.

From my interviews with Steve McCormack and the 'famous five' it is plain that they are really looking forward to the new era.

From conversations with other fans it seems that many 'lapsed' supporters will find their way back to the Stobart Stadium in 2008.

From the bottom of all Widnes hearts:

Thank you, Steve O'Connor, for saving our club!

STEVE O'CONNOR - A PROFILE

Although he is a committed life-long Liverpool FC supporter, Mr O'Connor has strong ties to Widnes, which is his birth place and home to his successful freight business founded by his family.

His father, Brian, started the O'Connor business in 1970, after leaving the Navy. He was very much a trucker at heart and when Steve and his three brothers and sister joined the firm after leaving school, the firm was running four trucks.

Steve O'Connor takes up residence at the newly re-named Stobart Stadium

From these small beginnings, he and his family have used their commercial energy and entrepreneurial flair to expand the firm into one of the UK's most successful haulage and logistics groups, incorporating rail freight, road transport and deep sea shipping.

Mr O' Connor said: "We run the most successful inland port in the UK at Widnes, moving thousands of tonnes of goods across the UK in a state-of-the-art logistics operation.

We have an honest and transparent approach to business and the vision and skill to deliver results. We have achieved this for our company and I strongly believe I can do this for the Widnes Vikings too.

"I am not in this for financial gain. The money is a gift, which will be managed by a Vikings' Trust Fund, but I want it to be used wisely and as a catalyst to attract other investors. The people of the town have helped to build our business and now I am delighted to be in a position to put something back, to leave a legacy and make a difference."

As a youngster, Mr O'Connor attended St Bedes Primary School in Widnes and recalls sneaking over the wall of the old Naughton Park ground by the toilets to watch the Widnes Rugby League team in action during the late '70s.

He played rugby league as a schoolboy, and although football is his first love, he is keen for his new club to win him over to the pleasures of rugby league. Mr O'Connor, who lives in Frodsham, Cheshire, is married to wife Clare and has three children Sarah, 23, Allen, 21, and Stevie, aged two. He is a man driven by success. As managing director, he transformed the O'Connor Group into a cutting-edge company, and recently sold his shares to Stobart Group in a multi-million-pound deal. He will continue to manage the operation and is now responsible for developing the Stobart brand across the North West.

CHAPTER ELEVEN

Factfile

APPENDIX I - RESULTS 2007

Date	Opponent	Comp	Venue	Score	Att
9th Feb	Celtic Crusaders	NRC 6	A	56-6	425
18th Feb	Leigh Centurions	NRC 6	H	34-20	4,133
25th Feb	London Skolars	NRC 6	H	60-10	2,760
4th Mar	Leigh Centurions	NRC 6	A	8-24	2,291
11th Mar	Normanton Knights	CC 3	H	78-10	1,606
18th Mar	London Skolars	NRC 6	A	66-0	789
25th Mar	Celtic Crusaders	NRC 6	H	32-10	2,540
1st Apr	Wigan Warriors	CC 4	H	24-34	6,006
5th Apr	Leigh Centurions	NL 1	H	46-12	3,792
9th Apr	Rochdale Hornets	NL 1	A	40-18	1,485
13th Apr	Sheffield Eagles	NL 1	A	46-4	1,211
22nd Apr	Batley Bulldogs	NRC-KO1	H	62-6	2,140
26th Apr	Halifax	NL 1	H	48-12	3,042
6th May	Batley Bulldogs	NL 1	H	66-14	2,753
17th May	Castleford Tigers	NL 1	A	44-20	6,007
27th May	Rochdale Hornets	NRC-Q/F	H	24-0	2,382
3rd June	Sheffield Eagles	NL 1	H	56-10	2,837
10th June	Doncaster Lakers	NL 1	A	90-4	1,248
14th June	Halifax	NL 1	A	6-12	2,142

24th June	Castleford Tigers	NRC-S/F	H	18-12	5,338
1st July	Rochdale Hornets	NL1	H	32-0	4,879
5th July	Dewsbury Rams	NL1	A	50-10	1,885
15th July	Whitehaven	NRC-F	N1	54-6	8,326
22nd July	Whitehaven	NL1	H	16-14	3,299
29th July	Doncaster	NL1	H	40-18	2,607
2nd Aug	Leigh Centurions	NL1	A	38-0	3,095
12th Aug	Dewsbury Rams	NL1	H	48-12	2,853
16th Aug	Castleford Tigers	NL1	H	18-24	4,598
2nd Sept	Whitehaven	NL1	A	22-18	2,360
9th Sept	Batley Bulldogs	NL1	A	34-18	1,139
20th Sept	Castleford Tigers	Q S-F	A	8-26	6,179
27th Sept	Halifax	E S-F	H	36-24	3,347
7th Oct	Castleford Tigers	Grand Final	N2	10-42	20,814

APPENDIX II - APPEARANCES 2007

	App	Sub	T	G	D/G	Pts
Bob Beswick	32	0	7	0	0	28
Damien Blanch	26	1	19	0	0	76
Adam Bowman	0	2	1	0	0	4
Andy Bracek	3	0	1	0	0	4
Darryl Cardiss	2	5	2	0	0	8
Mick Cassidy	17	11	1	0	0	4
Gavin Dodd	27	3	17	28	0	124
Lee Doran	23	9	5	0	0	20
Rob Draper	1	2	2	0	0	8
Dean Gaskell	16	4	11	0	0	44
Scott Grix	32	0	21	0	0	84
Ben Harrison	1	2	0	0	0	0
Jordan James	13	20	6	0	0	24
Andy Kain	9	0	3	0	0	12
Andy Kirk	12	5	8	0	0	32
Toa Kohe-Love	25	0	17	0	0	68
Danny Lima	0	5	0	0	0	0
Dennis Moran	28	0	23	0	0	92
Mike Morrison	0	3	0	0	0	0
Richard Myler	0	2	0	0	0	0
Mick Nanyn	29	0	28	161	0	434
Paul Noone	29	0	6	2	0	28
Joel Penny	14	1	10	0	0	40
Gareth Price	2	16	0	0	0	0
Adam Sidlow	0	4	0	0	0	0
Mark Smith	31	0	14	0	0	56
Aaron Summers	7	17	2	0	0	8
Joel Tomkins	8	0	2	0	0	8
Ian Webster	12	14	11	0	0	44
Oliver Wilkes	30	3	15	0	0	60

APPENDIX III - FINAL TABLES

Northern Rail Cup - Group 6

	P	W	D	L	B	F	A	Diff	Pts
Widnes	6	5	0	1	0	256	70	186	15
Celtic Cr	6	4	0	2	0	136	156	-20	12
Leigh	6	3	0	3	2	192	120	72	11
London SK	6	0	0	6	0	72	310	-238	0

National League One

	P	W	D	L	B	F	A	Diff	Pts
Castleford	18	17	0	1	0	860	247	613	51
Widnes	18	16	0	2	2	740	220	520	50
Halifax	18	12	0	6	2	616	421	195	38
Whitehaven	18	11	0	7	5	474	342	132	38
Leigh	18	9	0	9	4	454	474	-20	31
Sheffield	18	6	1	11	4	414	527	-113	24
Dewsbury	18	5	0	13	6	346	572	-226	21
Batley	18	5	1	12	2	372	645	-273	19
Rochdale	18	3	0	15	1	302	700	-398	10
Doncaster *	18	5	0	13	1	348	778	-430	10

* 6 points deducted for entering Administration

Appendix IV - Biographies

Bob Beswick   Loose Forward
Date of Birth: 08/12/84
Previous club: Wigan

Guitar playing Bob was a member of the 2006 National League One Dream Team, and declined Super League offers to remain with the Vikings for 2007. As vice-captain the Irish International formed a strong partnership with skipper Mark Smith, and was the launch-pad of many tries throughout the season. Bob was also an integral part of the Ireland team to qualify for the 2008 World Cup Finals, and later became one of the 'famous five' when he opted to remain loyal to the troubled Vikings for 2008.

	M	T	G	Pts
Widnes	64	13	0	52
Career	86	15	0	60

Damien Blanch   Wing
Date of Birth: 24/05/83
Previous clubs: Castleford, Penrith

Worth the entrance money alone to watch this flying winger in full flow. Damien, often the butt of dressing room jibes about his dress sense and arriving at training on his skateboard, originally joined the Vikings on loan from Castleford part way through 2006 before making the move permanent in 2007. A key figure in the run to two Grand Finals whilst at Widnes, his power and pace not only made him a favourite with the fans, it also persuaded John Kear to take him to Wakefield for 2008. Damien was another member of the Irish team that qualified for the 2008 World Cup Finals.

	M	T	G	Pts
Widnes	39	28	0	112
Career	51	32	0	128

Adam Bowman   Centre
Date of Birth: 12/11/87
Previous club: Widnes Academy

Local product Adam joined the Vikings in 2003 and progressed through the Academy structure, making his senior debut at Whitehaven in 2006 and earning himself a new contract for 2007. Limited first team opportunities led to him spending the last month of the season on loan at Swinton Lions where he helped to steer them to the NL2 play-offs. Adam returned to Widnes in time to represent the Senior Academy in their Grand Final defeat to Halifax.

	M	T	G	Pts
Widnes	11	2	0	8
Career	15	2	0	8

Andy Bracek   Prop
Date of Birth: 21/03/87
Previous Clubs: Warrington, St Helens

Andy made his senior debut with St Helens in the last match of 2004 before moving to Warrington for £22,500 in 2005.

His early season form was impressive while on loan from Warrington, but he was soon recalled following a spate of injuries at the Halliwell Jones Stadium, where he went on to score one try in five first team appearances in 2007. Andy was part of the Welsh team defeated by Lebanon in the World Cup qualifier at Widnes in November.

	M	T	G	Pts
Widnes	3	1	0	4
Career	27	3	0	12

Daryl Cardiss   Utility Back
Date of Birth: 13/07/78
Previous clubs: Warrington, Wigan, Halifax

Having been a near regular in 2006 this versatile, senior professional became a fringe player in 2007, and went on loan to Batley in July. The loan was cut short when he sustained a shoulder injury in only his second appearance for the Bulldogs. Darryl eventually moved on to big-spending Oldham Roughyeds for 2008.

	M	T	G	Pts
Widnes	31	12	0	48
Career	186	64	6	268

Mick Cassidy   Second Row/Prop
Date of Birth: 08/07/73
Previous club: Wigan

A Great Britain, and Irish International, Mick spent 14 years with his home-town club Wigan. He became an instant hit with Vikings' fans when he joined in 2005, and was Player of the Year in the relegation season. Although on a part-time contract for 2007, the word 'wholehearted' doesn't begin to do justice to his contribution to the cause. Mick moved on to Barrow in the close season, as well as setting up a World Cup Finals finale with Ireland.

	M	T	G	Pts
Widnes	82	6	0	24
Career	451	58	0	232

Gavin Dodd Fullback/Wing
Date of Birth: 28/02/81
Previous clubs: Oldham, Bradford

An attacking full-back who moved successfully to the wing in 2007 and became the Club's all-time record holder for points scored in a match with a return of 38 in the 90 - 4 win at Doncaster. Unlucky to miss out on selection for the Northern Rail Cup Final, Irish International Gavin returned to play a leading role in the march to the Grand Final. 'Doddy' was another Widnes player to help Ireland qualify for the World Cup Finals, and went on to achieve cult status as a member of the 'famous five'.

	M	T	G	Pts
Widnes	57	30	40	200
Career	195	90	40(1)	441

Lee Doran Second Row
Date of Birth: 23/12/81
Previous clubs: Rochdale, Oldham

Lee played in the same school team as Mick Nanyn. The two

linked up again at Swinton, and after each had a spell at Rochdale, became team-mates again at the Halton Stadium. Having almost destroyed the Vikings single-handedly in 2006 Lee became a firm favourite on his arrival at the club. Known as 'Tuna' - part of his staple diet - Lee in fact played a handful of games as an amateur for Widnes in his youth. The Irish International moved to local rivals Leigh as a result of the financial uncertainty at the club, prior to helping Ireland qualify for the World Cup Finals.

	M	T	G	Pts
Widnes	32	5	0	20
Career	201	46	0	184

Rob Draper   Second Row
Date of Birth: 30/11/87
Previous club: Widnes Academy

Having represented England Academy in 2006 Rob was expected by many to force his way into the first team squad for 2007, but Rob's season was beset by injuries which curtailed his progress. He spent a successful month on loan at Swinton Lions late in the season, helping them to the NL2 play-offs, before returning to Widnes to play in the Senior Academy Grand Final defeat to Halifax.

	M	T	G	Pts
Widnes	6	2	0	8
Career	11	2	0	8

Dean Gaskell   Wing
Date of Birth: 12/04/83
Previous clubs: Leigh, Warrington, Wigan

Despite undergoing surgery following his close season capture from Leigh Dean recovered to play a major role in 2007, as he went on to collect a Northern Rail Cup Winners' Medal for the second successive year. Having wrestled since childhood, and with Mike Forshaw while at Warrington, Dean believes this long-term hobby has benefited his tackling technique. Another member of the 'famous five', a fully fit Dean was looking forward to 2008 as pre-season training began, and hoping to re-establish himself in the Irish World Cup squad, along with cousin Mick Cassidy.

	M	T	G	Pts
Widnes	20	11	0	44
Career	109	34	1	138

Scott Grix   Fullback
Date of Birth: 01/05/84
Previous clubs: Leigh, Limoux, Halifax

Scott, another Irish international, followed Dean Gaskell from Leigh to Widnes, and like his team-mate picked up a winner's medal for the second successive year in the Northern Rail Cup Final. At his best Scott is an immaculate fullback with safe hands in defence who regularly displayed the ability to attack off either foot in scoring 21 tries in 2007. He joined fellow Vikings Damien Blanch and Ollie Wilkes at Wakefield during the close season, and partnered Blanch in Ireland's successful bid to reach the World Cup Finals.

	M	T	G	Pts
Widnes	32	21	0	84
Career	100	54	10	236

Ben Harrison   Prop
Date of Birth: 24/02/88
Previous club: Warrington

Ben joined the Vikings on loan with fellow Warrington Prop Andy Bracek. After promising early season displays he was also recalled to cover injuries at the Halliwell Jones Stadium, making four senior appearances for the Wolves in 2007.

	M	T	G	Pts
Widnes	3	0	0	0
Career	7	0	0	0

Jordan James   Second Row
Date of Birth: 24/5/80
Previous clubs: Wigan, Swinton, Sheffield, Castleford

'JJ' was initially brought up on Rugby Union and didn't switch codes until he was 21, following his stint in the Royal Marines. Having joined Widnes as a Second Row forward he was successfully converted to Prop for 2007 where he was part of a dominant unit, being one of only two 'ever-presents' in the squad. Jordan's final competitive action for 2007 was for Wales against Lebanon, at the Halton Stadium, before moving on to Celtic Crusaders for 2008.

	M	T	G	Pts
Widnes	48	10	0	40
Career	112	37	0	148

Andy Kain   Scrum Half
Date of Birth: 01/09/85
Previous club: Castleford

Andy became the latest to suffer from the poisoned chalice of the Widnes No. 7 shirt and found it difficult to produce his best form consistently. Loaned to Featherstone in late May for the remainder of the season, Andy was present at Headingley on Grand Final day, but in a Rovers shirt, as they clinched promotion to NL1. Andy made his move to the Chris Moyles Stadium permanent in 2008.

	M	T	G	Pts
Widnes	9	3	0	12
Career	68	29	45(2)	208

Andy Kirk   Centre
Date of Birth: 02/08/82
Previous clubs: Halifax, Wakefield, Salford, Leeds

A valued squad member, Andy had the unenviable task of competing with two of the most consistent centres in the League, but performed to a consistently high standard when he was called upon. In the past Andy's off-field activities have included being a part-time DJ and driving instructor, whilst he is known around the club for his 'Fred Elliot' impersonation! Andy will again be seen at the Stobart Stadium in 2008, but in the colours of Featherstone Rovers.

	M	T	G	Pts
Widnes	17	8	0	32
Career	114	52	0	208

Toa Kohe-Love Centre
Date of Birth: 02/12/76
Previous clubs: Warrington, Hull FC, Bradford

The 999th player to represent Hull FC, Toa made the short journey from Warrington to add his try-scoring ability to the Vikings' cause. His never-say-die spirit and tough tackling made him a firm favourite with the Widnes faithful. He picked up the first winners' medal of his senior career, in the Northern Rail Cup Final, in what was his 250th career appearance. Toa joined the exodus to Leigh Centurions at the end of the season.

	M	T	G	Pts
Widnes	25	17	0	68
Career	259	134	0	536

Danny Lima   Prop
Date of Birth: 27/07/75
Previous clubs: Wakefield, Salford, Warrington, Manly, Canberra, Sydney Roosters

Following a drawn out application for his work permit Danny failed to reach the standards he or his coach had hoped for. After struggling to establish a regular place in the squad he left the club after only 6 weeks and five substitute appearances.

	M	T	G	Pts
Widnes	5	0	0	0
Career	122	14	0	56

Dennis Moran   Stand Off
Date of Birth: 22/01/77
Previous clubs: Wigan, London, Parramatta

Dennis, who joined the Vikings on the same day as Jordan James and Oliver Wilkes, will be remembered for his trademark interception tries and formidable tackling. He was a member of the NL1 'Dream Team' in both 2006 and 2007 - the latter as NL1 Player of the Year. Despite a mid-season aberration of sporting a 'Mr T' beard, a clean cut Dennis collected the Supporters Club Player of the Year, and the Players' Player of the Year Awards in 2007. Having averaged nearly a try per game at Widnes he moved on to local rivals Leigh Centurions following the Grand Final defeat.

	M	T	G	Pts
Widnes	44	41	1	166
Career	307	170	35(6)	756

Mike Morrison Prop
Date of Birth: 09/08/87
Previous club: Widnes Academy

A promising Academy prospect, Mike made three early season substitute appearances and returned to the squad in the final weeks of the season without making the final 17. His progress and consistency was recognised when the Supporters Club voted him the Senior Academy Player of the Year, but he was another to make the short journey to Leigh at the end of the season.

	M	T	G	Pts
Widnes	3	0	0	0
Career	3	0	0	0

Richard Myler Half back
Date of Birth: 21/05/90
Previous clubs: Widnes Academy

Whilst still eligible for the Junior Academy Richard made his senior debut as a substitute in the final league match of the season at Batley, before making a brief but promising appearance at Castleford in the play-offs. One of the most disappointing effects of the off-field developments was Academy product Richard signing a three year deal with Salford.

	M	T	G	Pts
Widnes	2	0	0	0
Career	2	0	0	0

Mick Nanyn   Centre
Date of Birth: 03/06/82
Previous clubs: Whitehaven, Rochdale, Swinton

Having held a variety of records with each of his previous clubs Scottish International Mick became the club's record points scorer in a season with 388 in 2006. In 2007 he went on to increase that mark to 434 as well as setting a new record of 161 goals in a season. He won over his doubters in 2007 by adding a new powerful dimension to his defensive game in addition to his try-scoring and kicking abilities. With an average of 15 points per game whilst at Widnes Mick, known as 'Skids' in the dressing room, took his 'points machine' to Boundary Park when he joined Oldham in the close season.

	M	T	G	Pts
Widnes	55	58	295	822
Career	224	182	804	2336

Paul Noone   Second Row
Date of Birth: 22/04/81
Previous clubs: Harlequins, Warrington

A Former Great Britain Academy captain, Widnes born Paul realised a boyhood dream when he finally pulled on the Widnes shirt when Steve McCormack invited him to help take the Vikings back to Super League. Having played in a variety of positions for the Wolves, Paul immediately settled into the left-sided second row role for the Vikings, to produce a consistently high level of performance throughout the season. Paul, whose healthy year-round 'glow' is admired by many, played in his first professional Finals in 2007 and was, unsurprisingly, another to remain loyal to the cause during the dark days of the close season.

	M	T	G	Pts
Widnes	29	6	2	28
Career	166	20	28	136

Joel Penny   Scrum Half
Date of Birth: 22/01/80
Previous clubs: Doncaster, Halifax, Whitehaven, Manly, South Sydney, Cronulla

Joel was sanctioned by the RFL as Widnes' second 'quota' player for 2007 when he was released by Doncaster as a result of their own financial problems. Dogged by injury, Joel's performances were after a promising start, less dominant towards the end of the season. He returned to Australia at the end of the season.

	M	T	G	Pts
Widnes	15	10	0	40
Career	78	52	18(3)	247

Gareth Price   Prop
Date of Birth: 28/08/80
Previous clubs: Celtic, Hull KR, Rochdale, Leigh, London Broncos, St Helens

Gareth is another who has tasted both codes of rugby having turned professional at the age of 17. Whilst his performances grew in confidence and power as the season progressed, he failed to feature after the win at Leigh in August. Two months later he became the third member of the squad to join the Leythers when he signed a two year deal to return for his second spell at Hilton Park.

	M	T	G	Pts
Widnes	18	0	0	0
Career	137	21	0	84

Adam Sidlow   Second Row
Date of Birth: 25/10/87
Previous club: Widnes Academy

Adam made three appearances from the bench in 2007, before moving to Workington on loan in May. In a successful spell in Cumbria 'Big Bird' made a total of 18 appearances, scoring 9 tries, before returning to claim a place in the Vikings squad for the play-offs. His progress through 2007 persuaded Shaun McCrae to take him to Salford on a one year contract for 2008.

	M	T	G	Pts
Widnes	5	0	0	0
Career	23	9	0	36

Mark Smith   Hooker
Date of Birth: 18/08/81
Previous club: Wigan

After five years at Wigan Mark moved to Widnes in 2005 where he quickly became a crowd favourite with his strong and incisive play. 2006 saw him become the fulcrum of the team with 27 tries from 32 appearances and pick up the club's Player of the Year Award, in addition to being voted the NL1 Player of the Year. A born leader Mark was the obvious choice to take over as skipper in 2007, from the retiring Terry O'Connor, to lead his team to NRC success and another Grand Final appearance. A key member of the 'famous five'.

	M	T	G	Pts
Widnes	93	46	(1)	185
Career	216	58	(1)	233

Aaron Summers   Prop
Date of Birth: 11/08/81
Previous clubs: Whitehaven, South Sydney

Sydney born Aaron's two year stay at the Halton Stadium was blighted with injury, but he became a major force in the pack during 2007. Known for his 'red speedos' Aaron caused instant confusion among fans by dying his hair dark brown - a result of a dressing room bet - mid-way through the season. Defeat against Castleford was his third successive defeat in a Grand Final, and he moved on to Celtic Crusaders prior to winning a call-up to the Welsh squad.

	M	T	G	Pts
Widnes	48	6	0	24
Career	72	8	0	32

Joel Tomkins   Second Row
Date of Birth: 21/03/87
Previous clubs: Wigan

Joel came in on loan from Wigan at the end of July to increase competition in the pack, making a bright start and scoring an impressive try in his second game at Leigh. He returned to the Warriors at the end of the season.

	M	T	G	Pts
Widnes	8	2	0	8
Career	33	6	0	24

Ian Webster   Half-back / Hooker
Date of Birth: 16/11/86
Previous club: St. Helens

Ian spent much of the early season vying with Andy Kain for the No.7 shirt, but Joel Penny's arrival ultimately consigned him to 'the bench' from where he continued to make valuable contributions, including eleven tries in his first full season of senior rugby. At the end of the season he became the third member of the squad to join Celtic Crusaders, and also made his international debut when called up to the Welsh squad for the World Cup qualifiers in November.

	M	T	G	Pts
Widnes	26	11	0	44
Career	27	11	0	44

Oliver Wilkes	Second Row
Date of Birth:	02/05/80
Previous clubs:	Wigan, Whitehaven, Huddersfield, Leigh, Sheffield, Keighley

Much travelled Ollie rapidly became a fans' favourite with his barnstorming displays and never-say-die spirit. Like 'JJ' Ollie appeared in every match for the Vikings in 2007, as well as being part of the successful Scottish squad under Steve McCormack. In his most prolific season to date Ollie ran in 15 tries including a hat-trick in the 56-10 mauling of Sheffield Eagles. He reaped the rewards of his performances when he was offered Super League rugby by Wakefield Trinity in 2008.

	M	T	G	Pts
Widnes	47	17	0	68
Career	180	48	5	202

Steve McCormack   Head Coach

Thwarted in his attempt at a professional playing career by a serious shoulder injury at the age of nineteen, the former Great Britain Schools International turned his attentions to coaching with Wigan St Judes. After coaching the Salford Academy team Steve became Assistant Coach and then Head Coach at The Willows - at 28 becoming the youngest Head Coach to be appointed in Super League history, in July 2001. Leaving Salford midway through 2002 he took over at Whitehaven in January 2003 and led them to two Grand Final appearances, before accepting the challenge of leading the Vikings back to the top flight in 2006, again falling at the final hurdle. Following a successful Northern Rail Cup campaign in 2007 Steve took Widnes back to the Grand Final, in what was his

183rd match as a Head Coach, but was to see his team defeated for the fourth year running. Amidst the financial uncertainty that followed defeat against Castleford Steve's Widnes career seemed at an end when he accepted an offer to join Hull KR, but some 9 days later, and within 24 hours of Steve O'Connor buying the club, he was re-instated as Head Coach.

John Stankevitch   Senior Academy Coach

John amassed 131 matches, and 25 tries, in his playing career with St Helens before joining the Vikings for the 2005 season, where he added a further 22 appearances before injury brought an early end to a career that included England 'A' honours. He later had a successful spell as coach to the Senior Academy before accepting the Head Coach post at a re-formed Doncaster in June. 'Stanky' returned to his home-town club in December, as Assistant Coach, having resigned from his post at Doncaster some weeks earlier.

Tim Holmes   Senior Academy Coach

Following his enforced retirement after a promising, but brief, playing career Tim joined the Vikings' backroom staff. Midway through 2007 he assumed the mantle of coach to the Senior Academy when John Stankevitch joined Doncaster. Continuing the good work of his predecessor Tim guided his charges through to the Senior Academy Grand Final, where they eventually lost in a close fought encounter to a strong Halifax side.

Andy Haigh Conditioner

An injury-curtailed playing career which returned 27 tries in 89 games for St Helens, including Challenge Cup and Super League winners' medals, saw Andy join the backroom staff at Knowsley Road before finding his way to Widnes, via Wigan, in November 2005. Claimed by many in the dressing room to have the hardest accent to understand, Andy moved on to join his former coach Shaun McCrae at Salford following the end of season uncertainty at Widnes.

Samantha Whiteson Head Physiotherapist

Samantha joined the Vikings as Head Physiotherapist at the start of the year. Since qualifying as a physiotherapist at Liverpool University she has specialised in sports physiotherapy, and in particular both codes of Rugby. Sam brought a wealth of experience to the role having previously worked in private practice and with both the Sale Sharks and the North of England Under 18 team.

NB Player statistics refer to professional club careers only, and do not include representative matches at any level.

ISBN 142515860-9

9 781425 158606

against Halifax, and away fixtures at Castleford, Halifax and Leigh.

In a move designed to fit in with TV schedules the televised Play-off matches were moved from Sundays to Thursday evenings, although the Grand Finals would remain on a Sunday – October 7th 2007.

The greater exposure this afforded to the sport below Super League level was to be applauded. However, the fact that National League clubs featured in televised matches received no compensation from the broadcaster, for reduced attendances – unlike Super League clubs – was seen by many as the 'Sky tail' wagging the 'RFL dog'. It later came to light that the National League's new Sponsor was to 'pay' the home club £4,000 for each televised match – but even this had a sting in the tail as the clubs had to make a stipulated number of 'free' tickets available for each televised match. It is understood this virtually eroded the £4,000!

Points System

A new points system was introduced by the RFL for all National League competitions. This was reportedly an attempt to ensure more entertaining matches as teams would now be encouraged to play until the 80th minute in an effort to pick up a possible Bonus point depending on the margin of defeat. The first match to be played under these new rules was the Vikings' Northern Rail Cup match against Celtic Crusaders in Bridgend - although no bonus points were gained by the Crusaders!

Under the new system 3 points were to be awarded for a win; 2 points for a draw; and 1 point to a team losing by 12 points or less. A defeat by 13 points or more would still gain no points.

In support of this rule change the RFL posted the following rationale on their official web-site:

KEEPS GAMES ALIVE LONGER

By offering a tangible reward for strong, consistent performance over 80 minutes, the new system encourages teams to keep competing in games that they may not be able to win. To move the scoreboard in their favour, teams will play an attacking brand of Rugby League which will increase the spectacle and entertainment at many matches throughout the season.

ADDS AN EXTRA DIMENSION

The points system creates additional possible outcomes to games. Spectators have more to consider as they watch the action unfold. The system creates opportunities for clubs to take their destiny into their own hands and make a positive 'impact' on their League position. This will invigorate the competition tables in both the Northern Rail Cup and the National Leagues and will create greater levels of intrigue and excitement as the season progresses.

STRENGTHENS THE COMPETITION

The system encourages teams to be consistent and produce an optimum performance in all their matches throughout the season. This will stimulate individual players and teams to 'raise their game' which in turn will have a positive impact on the intensity and the on-field standards of the sport at this level

However whilst the RFL felt this would create greater levels of intrigue and excitement as the season progressed, fans were quick to realise that a team losing four matches - by 12 points or less - would gain more points than the team winning one game, and losing three by 13 points or more! Concern was expressed in some quarters that this seemed to devalue a 'win'.

When the season got underway the first Bonus point to be awarded came when Sheffield Eagles lost 18 - 20 at home to Doncaster Lakers in a Northern Rail group match on 16th

February 2007; whilst Oldham Roughyeds had the dubious honour of collecting the first Bonus point awarded in League competition. This was as a result of a 12 - 23 defeat at home to Featherstone Rovers in their National League Two fixture on Wednesday 4th April - the first National League match of the season.

After failing to claim a Bonus point from their Northern Rail Cup Group 6 defeat at Leigh in early March the Vikings went on an unbeaten run in national League competition until the narrow defeat in the televised game at Halifax (12 - 6) in late June. This was the first of only two Bonus points gained by the Vikings during the entire campaign - the second coming in the home defeat by Castleford.

For an analysis of the overall impact that this initiative had on the competitions in which Widnes competed turn to page 161.

Viking Starlites

A revamped pre-match entertainment programme for 2007 saw the locally formed 'Vikinettes' replaced with a troupe of professional dancers - the Viking Starlites - who appeared courtesy of SportStar Entertainment. Consisting of a mixture of professional dancers and students of dance and the performing arts, the company had an impressive CV which included the Super League Grand Final, Challenge Cup and Tri-Nations tournament, as well as performing at a host of rugby and football matches at club level.

In addition to providing pre-match entertainment Sport-Star extended their work into the local community, where they held weekly workshops at Stadium Fitness for local children aged 5 to 15, who became the 'Viking Starlets' who also performed at a number of matches throughout 2007.